BROWNLOW NORTH

BROWNLOW NORTH
THE ALL-AROUND EVANGELIST

Geoffrey Thomas

Reformation Heritage Books
Grand Rapids, Michigan

Reformation Heritage Books
2965 Leonard St. NE
Grand Rapids, MI 49525
616-977-0889
orders@heritagebooks.org
www.heritagebooks.org

Printed in the United States of America
19 20 21 22 23 24/10 9 8 7 6 5 4 3 2 1

Library of Congress Cataloging-in-Publication Data

Names: Thomas, Geoff, 1938- author.
Title: Brownlow North : the all-around evangelist / Geoffrey Thomas.
Description: Grand Rapids : Reformation Heritage Books, 2019. |
    Summary: "A biography of the Scottish evangelist, Brownlow North
    (1810-1873)"— Provided by publisher.
Identifiers: LCCN 2019031110 (print) | LCCN 2019031111 (ebook) |
    ISBN 9781601787170 (paperback) | ISBN 9781601787187 (epub)
Subjects: LCSH: North, Brownlow, 1810-1875. |
    Evangelists—Scotland—Biography.
Classification: LCC BV3785.N59 T46 2019 (print) | LCC BV3785.N59
    (ebook) | DDC 285/.2092 [B]—dc23
LC record available at https://lccn.loc.gov/2019031110
LC ebook record available at https://lccn.loc.gov/2019031111

For additional Reformed literature, request a free book list from Reformation Heritage Books at the above regular or e-mail address.

To my three God-fearing daughters,

**Eleri Brady, Catrin Alsop,
and Fflur Ellis,**

with the very deepest affection and gratitude.

Contents

Preface

How we need men who have been called by God to be evangelists! Yet we do not need "evangelists" characterized by the same theological and moral weaknesses found in many of the professing churches today. I am referring to the "snowflakes," those who by their lightweight preaching manipulate people into making easy decisions, who are self-promoting and self-advancing, who scarcely bother to mask their greed, who demand no evidence of new spiritual life in those they have touched. That sort of religion can never please God. Regardless of the intensity of brief tingle factors, it can never be blessed by Him.

But not so for the man equipped by an encounter with God, who is convicted of his own unworthiness, who has an unfading hope in the work that Jesus Christ has done, who trusts in the Savior's righteousness and His atoning sacrifice alone as his hope of eternal blessedness, who longs for everyone whom in providence he meets day by day to hear of this Jesus, who cries with every breath, "Behold the Lamb!" Such a man is characterized by a single eye that can provide eternal wisdom where hitherto there has been ignorance, the apprehension of mercy where there has been guilt, a protecting Shepherd where there has been impotence and vulnerability, and a longing for God where there has been the unsatisfied itch for worldly pleasures. What expectation we would have if we heard of such true servants of God being raised up in every part of the world in our generation. That would be the dawning of the time to favor us—yes, the set time. Then the churches in the most barren of nations would know that help centered on the Holy Spirit's energy and a new God-honoring life from heaven was coming to them. Alas, as it is, the absence of such graces in those who claim to be God's mouthpiece remains the chief cause of the church's moribund condition. The effects of this for the rest of the world are immeasurably calamitous.

Brownlow North is a crucially important figure—recent enough to be accessible and relevant to today's world yet representing a healthier time for the church. He was the model all-around evangelist, the archetypal definition of a New Testament preacher, the living embodiment of a man who has the conviction, "Woe is unto me if I preach not the gospel." His life displays what an infamous sinner can become when he has been transformed by being joined to Jesus Christ by faith through the grace of God. Knowing the terrors of the Lord, he beseeched men to turn and repent. He was a wise and courageous proclaimer, a humble interceder, a pastoral counselor, a churchman, a letter writer, an author, a theologian, and a redeemer of time. Human friendships were most important to him. One such friend, admiring North's unyielding convictions concerning important moral and theological issues, said, "When he believes something then 'not all the king's horses, nor all the king's men' could get him to discard it."

That was Brownlow North. He did not covet, abuse the weak and vulnerable, or exhibit laziness, yet he knew how to rest. For example, he enjoyed day excursions into the Highlands and onto the lochs of Scotland. He would go fishing with his son and with friends and played chess on many afternoons. He was full of liveliness and spirit, quick at repartee, entering into a burst of humor, especially if the fun was at his own expense. He amused children by imitating accents, and he listened to teenagers with warm sympathy. He was aware of his limits, knowing where to go and where not to go in many areas of his full life. He was characterized by manliness and intelligence, but chiefly with intense earnestness. He was a people person who loved his friends and kept in touch with them by constant delightful letters. He loved to sit in the company of such men as Dr. Alexander Moody-Stuart, Dr. Charles Brown, and Dr. Andrew Bonar. He sat at their feet like a child and delighted in what they taught him. Brownlow would spend his mornings in correspondence and writing his tracts and books, and in the afternoon he entered the drawing room with the family and joined in their occupations. He cared deeply for his mother, reverencing her, and he loved being with his wife and sons. They were not mere amusing illustrations for his sermons. He conducted family worship each evening, applying the truths of the passage with direction and sympathy.

His prayers were full and short, but direct as speaking to God. He believed that the judgment of hell was real and that it was a sin-hating God's response to all that contradicts His nature. He warned his hearers of God's judgment, often with tears, and some thought he wept too often as he preached. He told his hearers to count the cost of following Christ. He expected a new, transformed life of discipleship in every single man and woman of any age who made a profession of faith in Jesus of Galilee. New Christians were all to become involved in the prayer life, fellowship, burden bearing, and outreach of local congregations, however small. Led by Providence, they would themselves become growingly unashamed of the gospel, spreading the good news of the Son of God, who gives rest to all who would come to Him. They pursued the characteristics of a true Christian, as described by Jonathan Edwards:

1. He has a true knowledge of the glory and excellency of God, that he is most worthy to be loved and praised for his own divine perfections (Ps. 145:3).

2. God is his portion (Ps. 73:26), and God's glory his great concern (Matt. 6:13).

3. Holiness is his delight; nothing he so much longs for as to be holy, as God is holy (Phil. 3:9–12).

4. Sin is his greatest enemy. This he hates for its own nature, for what it is in itself, being contrary to a holy God. And consequently he hates all sin (Rom. 7:24; 1 John 3:9).

5. The laws of God also are his delight (Ps. 119:97; Rom. 7:22). These he observes, not out of constraint, from a servile fear of hell; but they are his choice (Ps. 119:30). The strict observance of them is not his bondage, but his greatest liberty (Ps. 119:45).

When Dr. Moody-Stuart (whose son became Brown-low North's biographer) met North, he soon found it "unspeakably refreshing to find a man with such a fear of the living God, such brokenness of spirit, and such faith in the everlasting Word." The providential meeting with Brownlow North became a great acquisition in his life, and it reminded him of Dr. Robert Reid Kalley on the island of Madeira, where for a long time there was only one convert. Finally, after more than a year or two, that solitary believer hurriedly came to Dr. Kalley and cried to him, "I have found a man!" There had been a second convert. As Dr. Moody-Stuart stated, "On the day I met Brownlow North it seemed to me that I had found a man whom God was redeeming to himself, was leading and instructing, and was sending as a labourer into his harvest."

I commend to you this man whom I more than admire and have also grown to love. If it were ever true of anyone, it is certainly true of Brownlow North, that to know him is to love him. May his life stir us, inspire us, melt our icy coldness, and make us more than stedfast and unmovable, abounding in the work of the Lord. It is not in vain that we should be wholly active in such laboring. May we know a personal rejuvenation through reviewing the life of this man of God.

Chapter 1

Early Years

Wee Kenny was the son of a fine gospel minister in Edinburgh, the Rev. Dr. Alexander Moody-Stuart. Father and son were very close, and one day the minister told Kenny that he had heard of the conversion of an English aristocrat up in the Highlands who had lived there for years, hunting, fishing, riding, and drinking, but now in his midforties (which was an elderly man in 1854) had turned from that lifestyle to take Jesus Christ as his own Lord and Savior. What is more, he had begun to speak about Christ to growing congregations of attentive men and women, many of whom made professions of faith and turned from their unbelief to trust in our Lord. There was an awakening in the north of Scotland. "So," said Rev. Moody-Stuart, "I have invited him to come to our church, Ken, and preach for some evenings for us." The young Kenny was very excited, and when he met Brownlow North, he was mightily impressed. He took every opportunity to hear him preach, and he often ate and drank with him in the manse.

Brownlow North died twenty years later, but during those two decades Kenneth Moody-Stuart had become a close friend, and he was the most suitable person to write a memoir of the evangelist's life upon his passing. It is a splendid biography, and I have read it often with delight and have used it extensively in this version of mine, which tells of how a rich man found greater riches than he could ever have imagined in the Son of God, Jesus Christ.

Brownlow North was born more than two hundred years ago on January 6, 1810. During this year, Beethoven would write his fourth symphony and violin concerto, the foundations of Dartmoor Prison would be laid, and Napoleon would expand his control of Europe. Within a few months of Brownlow's birth, Elizabeth Barrett Browning and Andrew Bonar would be born and William Pitt the Younger would die.

Brownlow's mother was distinguished for her deep Christian faith. In the Old Testament, Hannah had cried to God for a son, saying, "O LORD of hosts, if thou wilt indeed look on the affliction of thine handmaid, and remember me, and not forget thine handmaid, but wilt give unto thine handmaid a man child, then I will give him unto the LORD all the days of his life" (1 Sam. 1:11). Similarly, Rachel North's only child was the fruit of her intercession, and he became the focus of her prayers for the rest of her life.

Brownlow was a precocious only child, and one of the stories of those years (incidents that are preserved in every family) is of him as a five-year-old walking with his aunt, Lady Lucy North. Seeing some deer, he said to her, "Aunt Lucy, why are you like that big stag over there?" "I've no idea, Brownlow. I don't think I'm a bit like that stag."

"Because, Aunt Lucy," said the child, "you're a great dear." For that wit he was given half a crown.

He began his studies in Eton at nine and remained there for six years, leaving little impact on the school. However, he had begun to display some rebellious tendencies. When he was nineteen his father died, and Brownlow was sent to study at a theological college in Corfu. He was too wild spirited to remain there, and he soon returned home. He toured Europe with his personal tutor, but he paid little attention to new cities in new nations, learning nothing and marginalizing his tutor. He was much more interested in dancing, horse riding, and being in the company of women. One winter he proposed to no fewer than nineteen girls, all of whom accepted his offer of marriage! His horse riding developed until he became a kind of jockey, racing other aristocrats in places like Cheltenham. Serious accidents and deaths characterized some of those races.

After one such escapade, he went off to Galway, on the west coast of Ireland, to live quietly for a while. There he met a clergyman's eighteen-year-old daughter, Grace Anne Coffey, and he married her. By the time he was twenty-one, he had two sons to care for (eventually they were to have four sons, one of whom died in infancy). His income came from a position he was given by his grandfather, the bishop of Winchester. Brownlow was appointed the registrar of the diocese of Winchester and Surrey, and he took the duties of this post quite seriously, even though most of the work was done by a couple of lawyers. His salary was three hundred pounds a year, but this sum of money was insufficient to sustain his interest in horses. He became a gambler, losing much money and borrowing sums that he was unable to repay. He went to Boulogne to escape those demanding repayments, but his time in France was another totally fruitless escapade, and he sent his family home while he enlisted in the Portuguese army. That proved to be yet another debacle, and at twenty-five he returned to England, his life going nowhere. His family covered his debts, and he made the decision to visit his brother-in-law's home in Scotland to shoot grouse. He fell in love with Scotland and remained there for the rest of his life, becoming a virtually naturalized Scotsman.

For the next four years, he spent the summers shooting and the winters in a large house in the city of Aberdeen, during which time he raced horses and won many races. While shooting game in the summers, he walked energetically and tirelessly across the moors, exhausting all who tried to keep up with him. His motto was "Every day and all day." In one season at Glenbucket, he shot 770 brace of grouse in six weeks.

During these years the emptiness of this life would occasionally convict him, and he would kick against the goads of a troubled conscience. His mother's teaching and example could not be eradicated from his mind. He had Christian friends who prayed for his conversion, but none of his occasional seasons of repentance and new resolutions lasted very long. Once at a dinner party, he turned to a Christian lady, the Duchess of Gordon, and said to her, "What should a man do who has often prayed to God and never been answered?" She looked straight back at him and replied, "Ye ask, and receive not, because ye ask amiss, that ye may consume it upon your lusts" (James 4:3). Those few words made an unforgettable impact upon him; he became quiet that evening and was more thoughtful for some time. When his son Brownlow became very ill, he was further subdued and fearful. The Duchess of Gordon gave his wife a Christian book to read to the boy during his convalescence, but his father also read it and was convicted by its truths.

During the next couple of years, he experienced a temporary reformation of morals and began to consider training for the ministry. He went to Magdalen Hall, Oxford, and spent that time of study quite seriously. We know that from the fact that in his future books, beneath his name as author, can be found the words "Magdalen Hall, Oxford, and Registrar of the Diocese of Winchester and Surrey." Upon Brownlow's completion of the course, someone wrote a letter to the bishop of Lincoln, informing him of Brownlow's earlier excesses. When interviewed by the bishop, a spirit of casualness and uncertainty about his sense of call to be a minister surfaced. The bishop finally asked him, "If I were in your position and you in mine, would you ordain me?" "No, I wouldn't, my lord," he said.

What was his spiritual condition at that time? He certainly had a sense of his own guilt and shame; in fact, he would acknowledge with sadness that he was under the wrath of God. But there is a difference between admitting that one is a sinner and experiencing an inward divine change of heart. True repentance toward God is inevitably accompanied by faith in the Lord Jesus Christ. Looking back at his years of training in Oxford and his awakened conviction of personal sin, he judged, "I never apprehended Christ. I never accepted him as my sin bearer and my righteousness." He felt like the man in Jesus's parable who had swept and garnished his house and driven out the demon that had lived there, but he had failed to fill the house with the regenerating and sanctifying influences that come from the presence of the Son of God. The demons were hovering around Brownlow North, waiting to return in legion force. He later spoke of this state to a Christian woman, saying, "The house was swept and garnished, but empty, and the last state of that man was worse than the first. Think of the greatness of the love of the Lord Jesus which came to me after that!"

God used Brownlow's years of studying theology in Oxford to challenge his fine mind and deliver him from horse racing and shooting grouse. He was given some knowledge of the history of the church, especially of the Reformation and the Evangelical Awakening. He read and accepted the evidences of religion that Paley and Butler popularly provided in their books. These academic disciplines were not useless in his future ministry. For example, within a year of his conversion, he would be preaching to large gatherings, and he was glad of the grounding he had in the sweep of church history. He was aware of the rise of heresy and error, and he never had to withdraw words preached publicly or apologize for misleading or troubling the church. When he was considered to become a recognized evangelist in the Free Church of Scotland, his supporters could point out to its General Assembly that he had studied for the ministry in Oxford and completed the course.

But after years at Oxford had come to an end, he sadly drifted back to what he had enjoyed doing hitherto. At thirty-five years of age, he was again walking the moors of Scotland, especially around Inverness, gun in hand, month after month. As the time went by, he increasingly ignored God, silencing the voice of his conscience, and for three years he again simply shot grouse in the summer and rode his racing horses in the winter. His children got married, and when he was forty he settled in a large house in Dallas near Inverness, where he continued a totally secular life. His influence during those years was unhelpful to the kingdom of God, although he was always a kind and generous man. None of his friends cared anything for God, but he hated foul conversation. He said, "I never remained in the same room as a man who would encourage ungodliness and blasphemy." Yet what inconsistency he displayed, for on the Lord's Day he and his friends would ride off hunting, going past revived churches full of worshipers or Christian families walking to and from their meeting places. He would spend Sundays fishing for salmon. This is how he described this period of his life:

> For forty-four years of my life, my object was to pass time pleasantly; so long as the day was spent agreeably I was satisfied. During those years, whatever harm I may have done, I do not believe I ever did any real good to a human being. From 1835 until 1854, with the exception of about three years, the greater part of my time was spent in Scotland, where I rented moors and fisheries. My greatest idea of pleasure was to shoot grouse and catch salmon.

I believe, at the different shooting quarters I rented, I treated the poor with an average liberality, contributing to the different collections what I fancied would be expected, with an odd five shillings when an old woman lost her cow. What I considered my great act of kindness to the people, and that for which I expected them to be most thankful, was to give them, at the end of the shooting season, a dance and supper....

To this feast and party of mine all the tenants in the neighbourhood, with their wives and their daughters, were invited; as also the gamekeepers, the gillies, the shopkeepers of the village, my own servants, and all and sundry, and every acquaintance that any of them liked to bring. They were very merry. Late in the evening perhaps some were very noisy; and early in the morning I have seen some very tipsy. It would be daylight, perhaps, when a number of both sexes, would give me three cheers, and thank me for my kindness, and cry, "God bless you," and start on their ways home.

They thanked me for my kindness; but was it kindness? They cried, "God bless me!" but could either they or I expect God's blessing on such a meeting? It is true it was intended kindly, and was a return for kindness to those who had taken care of my shootings and preserved my game, and I knew no better way of saying, "I am much obliged to you." Yet again I ask, "Was it kindness?" In the end of 1854 it pleased God to bring home with power to my heart, that it would profit me nothing if I gained the whole world and lost my own soul.

Chapter 2

Conversion

During this period, Brownlow North's mother was still alive and more spiritually minded and prayerful than ever. She never ceased bringing him to God in her prayers. Other relatives, like his aunt, Miss Gordon of Wardhouse in Elgin, constantly prayed for him and thought about his mighty potential for the kingdom of God and his present wasted life. One day as she heard a sermon on the text, "Let me die the death of the righteous," Brownlow immediately came to her mind. She remembered much of the sermon, and when she got home she wrote him a letter with a full account of what she had heard. He read the letter and replied, "Dear Auntie, to die the death of the righteous we must live the life of the righteous, and I am not prepared for that yet." After he became a Christian, he would warn his hearers about his own defiance of God: "I said to God, 'I must have my sins; I know the consequences, but I accept them; I accept damnation as my portion.' I said that!" So his life continued until the autumn of 1854, when he was almost forty-five years of age.

In the summer of that year, he was still slaughtering

grouse day after day as if he were responsible for feeding Inverness. But there were those in his family who continued to pray for him, and throughout this time there grew an intensity and a burden in their prayers. Whenever Brownlow visited his aunt in Elgin, she would invariably ask him about his relationship with God. He said to her with typical insight and honesty, "I'm always saying things to you that make you think I'm promising spiritually. But I'm just giving you the impression that I'm better than I really am." However, there came an occasion on which he seemed to be heavier in spirits, for none of this shooting and sporting life was giving him lasting joy. He surprised his aunt by telling her, "I think I will go and see Blackwell."

Blackwell was his cousin, a preacher in the Church of England whom he admired and regularly visited. The minister was patient and kind with him. He was the man who was to introduce him to the concept of the grace of God— that it was not because of any of man's deserving or efforts but totally through God's mercy that a Savior had been provided for mankind in God's own Son. This man, Christ Jesus, lived the righteous life that all mankind has failed to live, and it was He who finally made atonement for sinners through the self-giving sacrifice of Himself on Golgotha. There He was made sin for favored men and condemned in their place as their substitute. And so the Father in His providence brings this message of the gospel into sinners' lives through the activity of preachers, friends, and family. Thus they are taught by God, and to them salvation is freely offered through Christ. God convicts them of its truth; He persuades sinners of their need of redemption; He gives them a new heart and faith to believe the gospel; He turns them from their unbelief to trust in Jesus Christ, and having begun this work in their lives, He continues to love them with His eternal love that will never let them go. Men at their best are what they have become by the grace of God alone. This was the message of the gospel that Brownlow North consistently heard from his cousin Blackwell.

Not long after Brownlow had visited his wife in Elgin, his aunt received a message from his wife informing her that her husband had been taken ill and that she believed his sickness was caused as much by his state of soul as his body. In fact, Brownlow had asked his wife to write this letter asking his aunt to come and visit him. So the favored time of his conversion finally came in 1854. Eight years later he was addressing a group of students in a Christian union at Edinburgh University, where he described what had occurred:

> It pleased God, in the month of November, 1854, one night when I was sitting playing at cards, to make me concerned about my soul. The instrument used was a sensation of sudden illness, which led me to think that I was going to die. I said to my son, "I am a dead man; take me upstairs." As soon as this was done, I threw myself down on the bed. My first thought then was, "Now, what will my forty-four years of following the devices of my own heart profit me? In a few minutes I shall be in hell and what good will all these things do me, for which I have sold my soul?" At that moment I felt constrained to pray, but it was merely the prayer of a coward, a cry for mercy. I was not sorry for what I had done, but I was afraid of the punishment of my

sin. And yet still there was something trying to prevent me putting myself on my knees to call for mercy,
and that was the presence of the maidservant in the
room, lighting my fire. Though I did not believe at
that time that I had ten minutes to live, and knew that
there was no possible hope for me but in the mercy of
God, and that if I did not seek that mercy I could not
expect to have it, yet such was the nature of my heart,
and of my spirit within me, that it was a balance with
me, a thing to turn this way or that, I could not tell
how, whether I should wait till that woman left the
room, or whether I should fall on my knees and cry
for mercy in her presence. By the grace of God I did
put myself on my knees before that girl, and I believe
it was the turning-point with me. I believe that if I
had at that time resisted the Holy Ghost—of course, I
cannot say, for who shall limit the Holy Ghost?—but
my belief is that it would have been once too often.
By God's grace I was not prevented. I did pray, and
though I am not what I should be, yet I am this day
what I am, which at least is not what I was. I mention this because I believe that every man has in his
life his turning-point. I believe that the sin against the
Holy Ghost is grieving the Spirit once too often.

The next day many were made aware of what the servant girl had heard and seen. Brownlow first told his wife
and children and the people staying in his house of his
change of heart and new trust in Christ, and then he took
pen to paper and spent the day writing to everyone, friends
and family, announcing to them that he had become a
Christian. Shortly after this his aunt, Miss Gordon, arrived
at their door, responding to Brownlow's wife's letter. She

found a new nephew, writing those letters to his family and friends, telling them of his conversion to Christ. He was quiet and gentle, and that evening at eight o'clock he came from his letter writing and joined the family in their daily worship. Brownlow North himself read a portion of Scripture and even made a few comments on it as if he had been doing this all his life. There was no hysteria at all. Then he prayed, finding in God his own pardon and peace. During the months that followed, he was often in prayer. He would at times stretch out on a rug with his mouth near the thin carpet, longing to be assured that the living God was hearing and answering him. He stopped smoking his cigars instantly (he had been addicted to nicotine), and he simply could not play billiards again. For months he read nothing but the Bible, not even the newspaper. The Crimean War was taking place, but he had no interest in its details. A greater struggle was taking place in his own soul.

Many of his friends at first greeted the news of his conversion with skepticism. It was suggested that he had had a breakdown, that it was a temporary excitement and that he would soon get over it. His withdrawal from his hunting and racing was reported in the newspapers, and some journalists wrote that he had done it all as a wager that he could gather thousands of people to hear him in a certain time. Christian people were also uncertain of this conversion, just as the early church doubted the conversion of Saul of Tarsus. He was one of the last people in the Highlands whom people expected to be converted. In fact, Brownlow North wrote on the margin of his Bible by Acts 9:21, "So it was with Brownlow North, and no wonder, and yet, for all that, he does believe that the Lord has spoken to him. To him be the gratitude and the glory." Then alongside the words of Festus to Paul in Acts 26:24, that the apostle was beside himself and was mad, Brownlow North wrote, "Christians in all ages have been called mad, but who was the most mad, Paul or Festus?"

Many old acquaintances either cast him off or hunted him down. They treated him as one dead to them and cast him out of their conversations as though he had ceased to exist or never had existed. Slanderous comments were made about him, but when they were traced very carefully, they were found out to be pure inventions or quite distorted stories. But many Christians who believed in the reality of conversion and had known his pilgrimage stood by him and encouraged him at this transformation of life. They were concerned when he set out by himself to visit some old friends who were not Christians and had fallen on hard times. As he traveled to help, they prayed that he would not be drawn away by these friends' contentment without God. But they were happy that his letters were full of encouragement. He would not travel on the Sabbath, and in a note to his aunt, he told her, "I have been twice to the Free Church in Inverness. I am being kept."

On a boat on the Caledonian Canal a little later, sailing to Fort William, one of the ship's stewards recognized him and was surprised at the different appearance of the man. Going north on that ship a few months earlier, Brownlow had consumed glass after glass of Scotch, but on this journey in the opposite direction, he seemed to the steward a broken man, leaning quietly on his staff, possessed by a seriousness and thoughtfulness. The next months were spent in that spirit. Like John Bunyan, who also went through radical conversion, Brownlow was becoming acquainted with his own heart. God was preparing him for evangelistic and pastoral ministry to the multitudes who would soon be coming to him with their spiritual conflicts. He became increasingly acquainted with deceptions in his own soul, but he also came into a stronger assurance that God was with him.

He had his own dilemmas, too, once telling a friend that he felt he could not pray for Christ to come again because he was far too afraid of the judgment. As they prayed together, his friend urged him to pray for the second coming. "I can't," he said. "I don't want it. I am fearful." "Then ask God to make you want it," his friend told him. That helped him as he thought of the atonement of Golgotha and how all his sins had been laid on the Redeemer and that when the Lord Christ returned, it would be as his Savior. So Brownlow could begin to pray, "Come, Lord Jesus." He was becoming a gentle and transparently honest man, finely tuned to help others.

He spent his first Christmas as a disciple of the Lord Jesus in 1854 with his mother, staying with her for a week. She could scarcely believe that her much-prayed-for only child who had been spiritually dead was now alive, that the lost one had been found. In the next months he came to a clearer understanding of the Christian faith, learning to hang for dear life on the things God promised in the Bible. He was encouraged to trust in the all-sufficient atoning sacrifice of the Savior for forgiveness of all his past sins, for cleansing all feelings of guilt, and for giving him peace with God. He learned to rely on faith alone as the means by which he could be joined to the Savior and all His benefits. He had many difficulties, but by going to the Bible frequently, they were resolved to his own peace of mind. On one occasion he said aloud to himself,

> Do you think by your own reason or deep thinking that you can find out God, or know Christ better than the Bible can teach you? If you can't, then why are you perplexing your brain with worse than useless speculation? Why aren't you learning from Scripture and holding on to what you've got? You must either make a god and religion for yourself, and stand and fall entirely and eternally on that god that you've made, or you must take the religion of Jesus Christ as revealed to you in his word. You cannot take a little of God's teaching and a little of your own. You cannot believe on the Lord Jesus Christ and the wisdom of your own heart at the same time. Choose then, now and for ever. By which you will stand or fall.

Then Brownlow put his hand on the open Bible and said, "God helping me…I will stand or fall by the Lord Jesus Christ…. I will put my trust in his truth and in his teaching as I find it in the written word of God…. Doing that, as sure as the Lord Jesus Christ is the truth I must be forgiven and saved." From that time on he submitted his intellect to the teaching of God's Word.

Three months after Christmas, he and his wife became members of the congregation pastored by Donald Gordon in the Free Church in Elgin. As he sat under the expository

sermons on the Gospel of Mark, his fears of condemna-
tion were calmed and his assurance grew. He was quite an
imposing presence sitting in the pew, with the marks of the
world's past conquests on him, an air of unrest, a strength
of will, a hungry look of need, a lowered head and a gazing
up with eyes fixed on the preacher. His posture could even
intimidate guest preachers. If they had not been prepared,
they would want to know about the intense man sitting in
the congregation. The minister set the needs of other members of the flock aside and often came and visited with him.

Brownlow continued to spend much time reading the
Bible. He never lost his wonder that the God of heaven
should have shown His mercy to the prodigal he had been.
But Satan's fiery darts continued to strike him. For some
periods he heard those whispers, "There is no God; there
is no God." They sounded in his ears unpredictably and
unwelcomed while he sat in meetings, or at times of personal prayer, or in the garden when he walked. He would
have to walk on, almost losing his reason, saying, "God
is; God is; there is a God." Even when going to a shop or
walking down the street on his way to some business, the
whispers would start again: "There is no God; there is no
God." This left its mark on him, but after coming through
such times, his conviction that God exists and that He
rewards those who diligently seek Him would give such
color and conviction to his preaching. His anchor verse,
where often he would cast himself, were these words: "Him
that cometh to me I will in no wise cast out" (John 6:37).
He quoted no verse from all the Bible more frequently in

his preaching and in his private counseling to anxious men and women.

At length, like Bunyan and Luther, North was delivered out of all his distresses and perplexities. He described his peace like this:

> I once had risen from my bed in an agony of soul, for I had been many months in trouble about my spiritual condition. I need not have been like that for many hours, if I'd only had faith to believe in Jesus Christ, and to make my own heart a liar; but my own heart told me that I was the chief of sinners, that Paul, who called himself the chief, was not to be compared—no, neither was he—to me, and that there could be no hope for me. For months I believed my own heart. One night, being unable to sleep, I had risen and gone into my room to read the Bible. The portion I was reading was the third chapter of Romans; and as I read the twentieth and following verses, a new light seemed to break in on my soul. "By the deeds of the law there shall no flesh be justified in God's sight." That I knew. But then I went on to read these words, "But now, now, the righteousness of God without the law is manifested, being witnessed by the law and the prophets; even the righteousness of God which is by faith of Jesus Christ unto all and upon all them that believe: for there is no difference." With that passage came light into my soul. Striking my book with my hand, and springing from my chair, I cried, "If that scripture is true, I am a saved man! That is what I want; that is what God offers me; that is what I will have." God helping me, it was that I took:

THE RIGHTEOUSNESS OF GOD WITHOUT THE
LAW. IT IS MY ONLY HOPE.

This period of satanic assault and of his searching for
assurance of forgiveness was an agonizing period in his life.
He once announced publicly that he would not wish his
worst enemy to endure what he had experienced. He also
said that his friends would tremble for him, thinking he
was losing his reason and that he would totally break down
under the strain of those times. It has been said that part
of the enormous influence he subsequently wielded in the
revivals of religion was due to the fact that for so long he
had served the world, the flesh, and the devil and then had
come to renounce all that. But the service of sin always has
bitter fruits and baneful consequences even though God
may bring some good from it. Habits can be formed that
injure the sinner himself. Brownlow North would compare
himself to the sick man of Acts 4 who was more than forty
years old when he received the miracle of healing. When
North began a new diary in 1855, the year after his conversion, he wrote these words after his name: "A man whose
sins crucified the Son of God." He then penned these words:

> Alas, that I so lately knew Thee,
> Thee so worthy of the best;
> Nor had sooner turned to vie Thee,
> Truest good, and only rest!
> The more I love, I mourn the more
> That I did not love before.

Chapter 3

Preparation to Become
an Evangelist

Eleven months after his conversion, Brownlow became convinced of his lack of compassion for the people of his district. He felt he must reach out to them with the gospel. But what could he do? Where could he begin?

Tract Distribution

Should he distribute tracts? Surely that would make him look ridiculous. People would laugh at him and call him mad, but he resolved to try, and one day he set out to a quieter part of Elgin with a pocket of tracts. He met an old woman and handed her a tract, which she took without a smirk. Then he offered one to another old woman who told him "Thank you" when she received it. Then the test came as a policeman came walking along the road. He offered one to him, and the constable said, "Thank you, Mr. North." For fourteen years he carried a supply of tracts in his pocket, and there was only one occasion when an atheist refused to take one.

However, there were others who avoided him, and Brownlow noticed this but took it as a cross he deserved to bear. This did not prevent him from engaging in conversation with people and leaving tracts in prominent places. He never found tract distribution easy, even after fourteen years. He said that it took him half an hour of internal struggle on a train journey before he offered a tract to a fellow traveler. Once he was traveling on a ferry and saw a group of gentlemen talking together. How could he speak to them? It was so pleasant and far easier to do nothing. This inner conflict went on for some time, but the feeling of eternal life facing these men galvanized him to act. He went across, and each one took a tract from him. Some of them knew him and would have been surprised if he had not acted as he did. Later on he wrote a number of very pointed tracts, such as the following:

COME!

You may think very little about the word "COME," and throw this paper away without reading it; but think of it as you will, be you sure of this, that of all the invitations you ever had, you never had an invitation so worthy of your attention. If you do not try and find out all about it,—who it is that says to you, COME, who you are invited to come to, and what you are invited to come for,—you are totally blind to your own best interests, and know not what you do. I tell you again, that of all the invitations you ever had you never had such an invitation as this, and that if you live and die without accepting it, your regret will be everlasting. Be wise then while you have the opportunity; and while I try and tell you, first, Who it is that says to you, COME; then, Who you are invited to come to; and then, What you are invited to come for; pay attention: do more than that. Take this paper home with you, and read it again there, dropping on your knees before you do so, and asking God for His Holy Spirit to bless it to you for Christ's sake. You will never accept the invitation, "COME," but by the Holy Ghost, but God will give His Holy Spirit to all *who* ask Him.

First, then, He who by the instrumentality of this paper now says to you, COME, is the God-man, the Lord from heaven; that He might be able to say it to you, He being in the form of *God* and who thought it not robbery to be equal with God, made Himself of no reputation, and took upon Himself the form of a servant, and became obedient unto death, even the death of the cross. The invitation to you now is quite free: it costs you nothing, you have only to accept it; but it cost the God-man, the Lord from heaven, more than you or I can understand, before He could say to you, COME. He was made man, made sin, made a curse, and forsaken of God; He was rejected, buffeted, spit upon, scourged, and crucified by man; He died, was buried, and was raised again, before He could say, COME, to one of the sons of men, and then ascend up where He was before. But He loved the sons of men, with a love that nothing would quench; so accepting the bitter cup; the agony and bloody sweat, the cross and passion, the death and burial, He drained it to the dregs, that He might be able to say, what He now can say, and does say, and says to you at this minute, COME.

Second, you ask—What does the Lord mean by COME: come to where, to whom, to what? Brother, it is to COME TO HIMSELF that the Lord invites

you: again and again is the invitation reiterated
in His Word, "COME UNTO ME." Now say not in
thine heart, Who shall ascend up into heaven to
bring Christ down to me? For God expressly warns
you against doing this; Christ is nigh unto you even
at this moment, but it is by faith that you must see
Him, not by sight. Without faith it is impossible for
you to come to Christ, for He that cometh to Him,
must believe that HE is; you must believe that HE
is, though you cannot see Him, and also that when
you come to Him He can see and hear you. Moses
was once exactly in the state of mind that I wish you
to be in at this minute. He desired to go out from
the world, and come to Christ. But how did he do
it? BY FAITH : see Heb. 11. 24. "BY FAITH Moses,
when he was come to years, refused to be called the
son of Pharaoh's daughter; choosing rather to suffer
affliction with the people of God, than to enjoy the
pleasures of sin for a season; esteeming the reproach
of Christ greater riches than the treasures in Egypt:
for he had regard unto the recompense of the reward.
By faith he forsook Egypt, not fearing the wrath of
the king: for He endured, as seeing HIM WHO IS
INVISIBLE." It cost Moses a great deal to come out
from Egypt, and you may expect that it will cost you
what you now think a great deal to come to Christ;
but as Moses was made more than conqueror, so
shall you be, if you come as he did by FAITH, and
endure as seeing HIM WHO IS INVISIBLE.

Thirdly, again you ask—For what does Christ
invite me to come? Reader, you have sinned, and
God has said, "The soul that sinneth it shall die." If
you have not the Son, no matter whether you con-

sider yourself a great or a little sinner, you have not LIFE but the wrath of God abideth on you; and if you die without having the Son, or in other words without having come to Christ, that wrath will abide on you for ever, and then good would it have been for you if you had never been born. But Christ invites you to come to Him, that *you may have* LIFE. It was for this that He lived and died and rose again,—that He might have power on earth to forgive sins, and give *eternal life* to every one that comes to Him. As a lost sinner He now asks YOU to come to Him, and He tells you before you come that He has power to save to the uttermost them that come. Moreover He tells you to "come boldly"—that is in faith, and nothing doubting—for that him that cometh to Him He will in no wise cast out.

And now what are you going to do? Will you accept His invitation and come to Christ, or will you continue to walk in your own ways? Remember it is not more true that Christ Jesus came into the world to save sinners, than that He now says to you "*Come unto Me*" and that if you come He will receive you. There is a day coming when He will say "*Depart*"; but He never said it, and never will say it, to mortal man on earth. The whole Bible is one great call to COME, and he that comes is saved.

Sick Visitation

As a member of the Free Church of Elgin, he was introduced to sick members of the congregation and began to visit them. Another church member recalled such visits:

I remember his supplying the very poor and bedridden with many little comforts, such as introducing gas into their cheerless rooms, and paying for it himself. I have myself gone with him to see some of these poor creatures and I shall never forget some of these visits, one in particular, to a poor wretched old body who had been unable to leave her bed for years. Mr. North would take a little stool, sit down at her unlit fire, and peel oranges for her and all this in a room where the surroundings were too disgusting even to mention. After that time, I for one felt that I couldn't be in his company for a quarter of an hour without benefiting from it. We all loved him much.

In addition to visiting people in their homes, he was invited by a town missionary named John Gow to accompany him in visiting the patients in Gray's Hospital, which he did regularly on Sunday afternoons.

Evangelistic Visitation

From visiting the sick, there naturally developed evangelistic visiting. Once, in Aberdeen in January 1863, Brownlow spoke of this step, drawing a contrast between the promptings of the flesh and the promptings of the Spirit:

When I first came to know the Lord, the Spirit said to me, "Brownlow North, there's that woman in the porter's lodge; you ought to go and speak to her about religion." But the flesh said, "Do nothing of the sort; keep what you've got to yourself." But the Spirit gave me no rest till I went to the woman at the porter's lodge, and read the Bible to her, and told her what the Lord had done for my soul. Then again the Spirit said to me, "There's the washerwoman in the town, you know; you should go to her, and read and pray with her also." But the flesh said, "Do nothing of the sort; she will likely think that she has more religion than you have." Still the Spirit would give me no rest till I read and prayed with the washerwoman also.

So he gave away tracts and visited the sick, reading the Bible to them and occasionally praying.

Personal Conversations

A woman wrote to North from Torquay, knowing that he was going to London, and asked him if he would visit her son, a colonel in the Scots Guards, and talk to him about his soul. He reacted against such a request immediately: to intrude on a man he had never met, while the woman was only slightly known to him—what was this? He kept the letter in his pocket, but it was burning a hole there! At last he determined to visit the man, whom he found to be tall and handsome with a long beard and fashionable dress. "Colonel, I have come to you on what you will think is a strange errand. I am Mr. North. I had a letter from your mother recently asking me if I would call on you and speak with you about your soul." "Ah, you are Mr. North. My mother wrote to me and informed me that I might have a visit from you. Sit down on the sofa." So he did, speaking to the soldier about eternity and the work of Jesus Christ, urging him to leave the world and cleave to the Savior. "But," Brownlow continued, "you must do this out and out, and not be ashamed of it. Go to your club or to your mess and tell them you have a new Master." The colonel shook his head. "I daresay that you shrink from it. You would rather lead a forlorn hope or brave any military danger, but let me assure you that telling men of your trust in God is not as difficult as it seems at a distance. The lion is chained. I am myself proof of this. I recently got a letter from a lady whom I barely know. She asked me to go to a Colonel of the Guards whom I had never seen, and speak with him about his soul. If you had got such a message, you wouldn't have liked it." "No," agreed the Colonel, "I should not." "Neither did I. In fact I felt like rejecting your mother's request out of hand, as I thought that you would have treated me in that same way. But I came and you treated me like a gentleman. You entered frankly into conversation with me, and I am ashamed of my timidity." The colonel was pleased with his response and later came to hear Brownlow at a London meeting.

Brownlow once met a famous actor whose name was Charles Kean. Many people thought that the two men looked alike. He invited him to come to one of his meetings, but the actor defiantly replied that he could not if he would and he would not if he could. It is through many such conversations that he learned to speak wisely and intimately to men and women. He was as fearless as a lion in rebuking any levity on Bible subjects or any approach to profanity. He did not care who the offender might be or what was his position; Brownlow spoke out.

Occasional Public Speaking

He once was visiting a young woman whom he had been told about. She evidently did not have long to live, and she said to him, "Oh, don't mind me, please go to my father and speak to him, for he's a bad man." Brownlow obeyed and spoke to her parents, who were impressed by what he said. Two other people were in the room, and they were helped by his words so much so that whenever he visited the home (which was very frequently in order to see the dying daughter), they returned to hear him. The father was changed, and the news of his new life spread through the neighborhood. After that, many more people pressed into the house when Brownlow North visited the girl.

Then a woman came to him and asked him to speak to her husband "just as you are speaking here," which he did. The man was a shoemaker, and he asked Brownlow to return to speak to some of his work fellows. A dozen shoemakers gathered to hear him, and they asked him to return. This time sixty men assembled to hear him. These meetings increased in size and in various locations so that soon Brownlow North was speaking every night in cottages all over Elgin, and one evening two hundred people met in a granary to hear him. There was a solemnity and deep hearing of his message. In fact, the daughter-in-law of the Rev. John Macdonald, the "Apostle of the North," heard about these meetings and tried to attend one, but she could only sit on the stairs outside a hired loft because it was so full. Many were turned away. She heard his preaching without seeing him, and she said that she had heard nothing like it since she had listened to her mighty father-in-law preaching.

He would be taken home by one of the elders of the church, and often on that journey, Brownlow would express his fear that he was going beyond the line of duty in speaking at meetings like that, that he was trespassing on the duties of the minister. But he could find no definite prohibition stopping him from accepting the invitation to speak to men and women about the gospel. He spread the matter before God in prayer, again and again asking Him that if this exhorting were against God's will that He would close this door, but the very opposite occurred: invitation after invitation came to him to speak to gatherings of men and women.

Brownlow's preaching came out of his love of people. There developed a readiness to travel and visit men and women who had been commended to him by their Christian families or friends as having particular needs. Sometimes this entailed traveling across Scotland with no assurance at journey's end that his presence at their front door would be welcomed. If he could not see them, he would write a long letter to them. Once, as a guest in Moody-Stuart's home, the minister noted the length of time the evangelist spent writing one letter to a man whom he had known in his earlier life. Brownlow's influence at that time had not been helpful. He was conscious of his earlier failings and so wrote at length to this former companion with the hope that his words might draw him to the God he had come to love. A Christian wrote to him asking if he would visit her brother, a man he had hunted with in his early life. Brownlow shrank from the invitation, but she gave him his address in Edinburgh, and so reluctantly he went to the city to see him. Upon arriving he discovered he had lost the piece of paper on which his address was written, so he took a cab to the station to go to Glasgow. In the cab he put his hand in a pocket and found the address. Immediately he ordered the cabby to drive him there. It would have been so easy to plead the change of plans, but that was not Brownlow North. He went to see the man and addressed him earnestly and lovingly.

Street Preaching

North's street evangelism commenced after he had gone to London to visit his mother. One Sunday afternoon he called on a young Scotsman who had been converted in a remarkable way and, filled with love for God, had begun to preach in the street. When North called on him, he was about to go preach on the streets around King's Cross, and he asked Brownlow to accompany him. He stood on a street corner, prayed, and then addressed a handful of people. No one stopped; his words made no impact on the passersby, and there was a sense of frustration in the air. Then some of the people started to shout out, "We'll hear the stout man with the dark eyes." There was no escape, and Brownlow North, there on the street corner near King's Cross, began to preach. Immediately people stopped and gathered. Their attention was riveted on him, and he preached until he was exhausted. Many voices cried out, "Go on! Don't stop," but he was physically unable to preach any further. Thus, without any premeditation, Brownlow was persuaded about the usefulness of open-air preaching, about his own ability to speak on such occasions, and about God's presence as he preached.

Sunday Preaching from the Pulpit

Again Brownlow was directed into this through a providence that was completely out of his control. He returned to Dallas, where he had spent many years hunting and fishing and racing. He was welcomed, and he told the people of the local congregation that he was looking forward to being in the Free Church on Sunday. They told him that their minister had been called away and that they could find no one to fill the pulpit. Unless he preached, there would be no sermon. They pleaded with him to speak. He pointed out that he had not been ordained, but they thought these were unusual circumstances. He reluctantly agreed as long as an elder took the devotions and called on him to give an address. That is what transpired, and the people listened, thinking of all that Brownlow had been in this community and what God's grace had affected in him during the previous eighteen months.

The next day there was a terrible tragedy in the community. The river was in flood, and two children who had tried to cross it on a plank were drowned. The village was plunged into mourning, and the minister was away; the father came to Brownlow and asked him to come speak to his wife. While he did so, the children's bodies were brought back to the cottage, accompanied by most of the community. Brownlow stood outside the home and addressed the people, following on from what he had said the previous day, urging them to prepare to meet God. Soon the minister returned and heard all that had transpired, and he urged Brownlow North to preach again in the church. This time the building was full.

Among the congregation were two men from eight miles away, who returned to their community with a glowing report of what they had heard. Within a couple of days, a deputation came asking him to preach in their church. Again Brownlow raised his objections about not being ordained, but they would not take no for an answer. The first night he preached, there was a large and attentive congregation; the next night every seat was taken, and even the staircases and doorways were filled with anxious people. People were converted, and the cause of the gospel was revived in that place. The church was changed after those meetings.

When later he was asked to explain whether he was a "real preacher," he would say something like this: "Don't think that I'm intruding into the office of the ministry. I am not an authorized preacher, but I'll tell you what I am; I'm a man who has been at the brink of the bottomless pit and has looked into it. Now I see many of you going down to that pit. I am here to 'hollo' you back, and warn you of your danger. I am here, also, as the chief of sinners, saved by grace, to tell you that the grace that saved me can surely save you." It is significant that in Dallas, the place where he had so publicly shown his opposition to the claims of Christ, he began preaching on the Lord's Day and in a place of worship, which for the rest of his life, he did so tirelessly and to such great effect. It was there that someone asked him what he intended to do in the future. He replied, "I have done all the harm I could in Scotland, and now I intend to remain here and do all the good I can."

Raising Support for Other Local Evangelists

Brownlow North approached John Gow and invited him to become a Scripture reader in Elgin, which he accepted. He visited houses and held meetings for the next twenty years, just as Brownlow had been doing. A Christian banker named Robert Brander, who had been touched by this outreach and Brownlow's ministry, gave a sum of money, the interest from which was set aside to support the town missionary. So, very easily and sweetly, doors were opened, invitations were made, and others were drawn into this work of spreading the good news of the Lord Jesus Christ.

This was the remarkable beginning to Brownlow North's life in Christ, even though it was not unique among other evangelists in history. He was marked by a seriousness of attitude and a spiritual consecration from the very beginning of his work. You cannot understand him unless you have grasped that this spirit was the energy of his whole life. One of his favorite verses was Colossians 3:17, "And whatsoever ye do in word or deed, do all in the name of the Lord Jesus." That was the touchstone by which he sought to prove every action. When people sought his advice on Christian living, he would ask, "Can you do it in the name of Jesus?"

Such a grueling schedule of visiting and preaching was thrust on him that he finally collapsed and saw a doctor, who made him cancel all his engagements for a few months. He went to the village of Arndilly to recuperate, and as he got better he was tempted to do a little fishing again. He asked his Christian friends what they thought, and their response was that if he was unable to fish for men at that moment, it might be a good thing for him to fish for fish. It might even aid his recovery to fish for men. "I'll go to my room and ask the Lord Jesus Christ to come with me," he said. "Unless I feel persuaded that he will go with me, I won't go." He wrote about this fishing dilemma in a letter to Alexander Moody-Stuart:

My very dear brother,—I have just got your dear kind letter, and will not go to bed without writing a line. You remember our conversation about "fishing." Well, after much thought and some prayer, I felt it was bondage not to go. I felt sure it would do me good, and out I went. With every cast of my rod I seemed to improve in health. The first day I killed a fish—second day none—third day, engaged a man to come with me, and going out about four in the afternoon we killed six (I four and he two), and walked and felt a new man in mind and body for vigour and spirits. Fourth day, started after dinner, about four. Going down a steep bank, I slipped, and broke a sinew in my leg, and was brought up the brae on a man's back, and home in a donkey chair! From that first moment I was able to say, "It is the Lord," and to praise Him, and I am sure all this was His hand in love. I could not fall to the ground without His will, and I felt it was His will to stop the fishing, perhaps; but of this I am not clear. I have now been laid up a week, with my leg in a thing that keeps it bent, and in a few days I hope, with the help of a high-heeled shoe, to hobble about. Oh, do pray for me, that whatever the Lord would have me to learn, He will send His Holy Spirit to teach me for Christ's sake; for if He does not, though the book is put before me in the shape of "accident" or what not, I shall learn

nothing aright. I got much pleasure out of Romans
viii. 28 and 32 the other day: "We know that all things
work together for good to them that love God," etc.
These things are all so literally true and real, or else
there is no truth in any part of God's Word, and as
that is not true, it follows all is true. And oh what joy
and peace thus to receive it!... Oh to be unselfish and
single-eyed! Pray for me.

Brownlow North

Arndilly, August 9th, 1860

There was some discussion about a man setting out to
preach so soon after his conversion. Should he have lived
in seclusion for some years before speaking? A whole year
did pass before he began the ministry God gave him, but
as you examine the history of his early years as a disciple of
Christ, each step of the way seems to have been marked out
by God. There was no plan formulated by Brownlow. He
gradually, reluctantly, and unexpectedly became a preacher
of the gospel. Before he preached he was weighed down
with a sense of the responsibility that was now his; there
was a heaviness on him for some hours before the service; a
dispensation of the gospel was committed to him. It would
be woe to him if he preached not the gospel. He never dis-
charged those duties in a light-hearted manner. Certainly
there was widespread knowledge that this infamous man,
Brownlow North, who had spent many years in rejecting
the gospel and defying the Bible, had now been converted,
and so many were moved to hear him. Others opposed him
strongly from the beginning, yet Brownlow handled it humbly. K. Moody-Stuart related one unforgettable incident:

One evening Mr. North was about to enter the vestry of a church in one of our Northern towns in which he was going to preach, when a stranger came up to him in a hurried manner, and said, "Here is a letter for you of great importance, and you are requested to read it before you preach to-night." Thinking it might be a request for prayer from some awakened soul, he immediately opened it, and found that it contained a detail of some of his former irregularities of conduct, concluding with words to this effect: "How dare you, being conscious of the truth of all the above, pray and speak to the people this evening, when you are such a vile sinner?"

Brownlow North put the letter into his pocket, entered the pulpit, and after prayer and praise, commenced his address to a very crowded congregation; but before speaking on his text he produced the letter, and read to the people its contents. Then he added, "All that is here said is true, and it is a correct picture of the degraded sinner that I once was; and oh how wonderful must the grace be that could quicken and raise me up from such a death in trespasses and sins, and make me what I appear before you to-night, a vessel of mercy, one who knows that all his past sins have been cleansed away through the atoning blood of the Lamb of God. It is of His redeeming love that I have now to tell you, and to entreat any here who are not yet reconciled to God to come this night in faith to Jesus, that He may take their sins away and heal them." His hearers were deeply impressed by the words he spoke, and that which was intended to close his lips was overruled to open the hearts of the congregation to receive his message.

So he continued to preach day after day, accepting every invitation he could to tell of his Savior, rarely complaining of tiredness in the Lord's work. He said, "The feeling of life is not to be cherished. We should not desire it to be shortened, for we do not know how much we owe God for every day of patient continuance in well-doing, or how much each day is adding to our eternal blessedness."

Chapter 4

First Years of Ministry

News of his ministry and God's blessing on it spread across Scotland. Early on he preached in Huntly, where once he had stubbornly lived as a rebel against all things Christian. The attendance was enormous, and emotionally he was overwhelmed. He stood up and faced the people, breathed deeply, and said, "My friends, you all know me. You know how I lived at other days, but God…" He could go no further, sitting down and burying his face in his hands. Twice more he arose and sought to speak to them but was utterly unable to do so, and the meeting ended without any preaching. Finally he rose and prayed, thanking God for His mercy to them all. It had been twenty years since the revival in Dundee under William Burns. Many remembered those days and saw the same work of God convicting the careless of their sin and giving assurance to those who sighed, "I believe; help thou my unbelief." He preached in many of the churches in Morayshire. Brownlow went further to Fort William and Lochaber, preaching with power and creating a deep impression among those who knew him. Then, further afield again, he preached in different churches in

Inverness; Forfar; Aberdeen, where he preached in Gilcomston Church in December 1856; and Montrose. Wherever Brownlow preached, God accompanied the Word with awakening power, and congregations of every denomination who loved the truth received him with thanksgiving.

While listening to North's preaching in Gilcomston, a woman who had made her profession of faith two weeks earlier was greatly touched, and her account of his preaching and counseling is striking:

> I was struck and startled with the faith of his first prayer. I thought, What is my religion worth? I can't say "Father" to God, as that man does. His text was Acts 17:12, "Therefore many of them believed." There was much of the power of the Holy Spirit with him that evening; and as he went on it was all to me so tremendously real and present. I felt as if I had never believed before that the Son of God really came down and died for sinners. At the close he entreated us all most earnestly to speak to Jesus there and then. He cried, "O, speak to Him! If you can say nothing else, tell Him you hate Him, but speak to Him as you are." I remember well hiding my face in the pew, and saying that to Him in deepest grief, and begging Him to change me.
>
> Next Sabbath his text was Proverbs 1:20–33. In opening up the clause, "Fools hate knowledge," he brought together one after another of the Bible descriptions of fools, and applied each most impressively; e.g., the atheistic fool of Psalm 14, the rich fool of Luke 12, the self-confiding fool of Proverbs 28, and the backsliding fool of 2 Peter 2. He described the backslider, and said, "You are only a fool after

all, and now Christ is saying to you, 'Turn you at My reproof, behold I will pour out My Spirit unto you.'" Then I broke down, and turned to Christ to beg to be received, and to ask His Spirit.

The following evening my two friends and I went to his lodgings at the hour when he intimated he would be at home. He prayed with us first, then spoke pointedly to each, setting Christ before us from Romans 3:21–26, in His righteousness and death and power to save. He gave us Christ's invitations and promises but we could not believe. I asked, "Has one a right to believe that Christ loves one personally?" He answered quickly, "If you don't believe that, you will go to hell," and read to us 1 John 4:16, "We have known and believed the love that God hath to us." He asked, "Are you willing to forsake all for Christ, to give up the world, its pleasures, companionships, etc.?" and rapidly grouping up a list of trials for Christ, he asked me in his own direct, forcible way, "Could you bear that?" and I said, "I think I could." He answered, "You remember Peter, he thought he could, and what did he do?" He put the same question to J. F. She did not answer at once, and he said, "Remember, it is not to me that you say it, but as you must answer at the judgment-seat of Christ." She answered "Yes," very solemnly, and Mr. North turned to her younger sister, M. F., with the same question. She answered "Yes," and he added, "Remember the young ruler." He said, "Don't expect to be perfect Christians in five minutes: you must be babes first, and then grow, feeding daily on the Word." He spoke with evident delight of some of the rich portions of the Word, and said, "Isn't that food?" He talked with us of pardon, and acceptance, and victory over sin, and the welcome at last, "Well done, good and faithful servant," and bade us meet at least once a week to read and pray together, which we did for some years, till our paths in life separated. The servants came a second time to say that many more were waiting to be spoken with, and warning us not to lose our convictions he bade us farewell saying, "God bless you, dear sisters."

One basic principle by which he counseled people was that it was erroneous to exhort people to conquer their corruption before they had addressed their unbelief and sought Jesus Christ as their Lord and Savior. He said that the devil is the one who seeks to focus people's attention on their failures; he is the one who suggests that if they could first put to death their sin, then they might trust in Jesus. The Scripture's counsel is the very reverse: believe on the Lord Jesus Christ and be delivered from the domination of sin.

The effect this preaching had in Scotland was altogether electric. North stood before the people in the prime of manhood, forty-six years of age, distinguished looking, educated, built like Luther, deep-chested and broad shouldered, deadly serious, in earnest about all he said, naturally eloquent and fresh in his approach to Scripture, a man of dignity and gravity dressed in dark clothes. A minister who had known him before his conversion and had heard that he was a changed man and had become a preacher said, "Well, if he is to do any good he will require a reformed face as well as a reformed life," and that certainly happened. Dr. John "Rabbi" Duncan once commented on a photographic likeness of Brownlow, saying, "There is intellect in the brow, genius in the eye, and eloquence in the mouth." Before listening to him, that generation in Scotland had not heard such evangelistic preaching. Through his ministry, hundreds of men and women, old and young, were awakened and given assurance that they had peace with God.

Chapter 5

His Preaching and Praying

In his opening prayer, Brownlow North would draw the congregation into God's presence. The spirit of reverence and godly fear that characterizes each revived congregation was mightily upon his ministry. At one meeting in Elgin in the year 1862, someone transcribed his pulpit prayer in shorthand. This is how and what he prayed:

> Lord God Almighty, Thou who dwellest in the heaven of heavens, Thou who revealest to us that "Wherever two or three are gathered together in Thy name, there Thou are in their midst," O God, help us to pray! We have stood up before Thee in the attitude of prayer; we have ourselves invited Thine attention by our own act and deed in coming unto Thee; we have called upon Thee specially to regard us at this moment; and O God forbid that, when Thine eye is turned upon us, Thou shouldest see a single heart amongst us that is not endeavouring to pray. It is so hard a thing to pray, that, except Thou pour upon us the spirit of grace and supplication, we never shall pray. O God, before we can pray we must feel want; we must feel that we are poor and needy; O grant us then to feel our need! Grant us that hungering and thirsting

which Thou hast promised to satisfy. O God, unless Thou create the desire, there will be no desire, for the natural man desireth not God. Is it witnessed of us all in heaven, "Behold he prayeth"? Thou knowest, Thou knowest. O God, if there be one here who is not praying, we, Thy praying people, remembering Thy commandment to love our neighbour as ourselves, would join as one man and pray for the prayerless. We pray to Thee, O God, we who do pray, pray to Thee to make the prayerless pray. May the prayerless be compelled to smite upon their breasts, and cry, "O God be merciful to me." May they join now, O God, with the praying ones, and may there not be one here of whom it is not witnessed, "Behold, he prayeth."

Now, Father, we want everything; we want Thee to take away from us all our own things—everything we have got, so that we may have nothing we can call our own, that all those things which we have by nature may pass away. Then we pray that all things may become new, and that all these new things may be of Thee. And then we pray to Thee, Father, that, being led by Thy Holy Spirit, we may sacrifice to Thee all Thine own. We pray that we may have faith that we may have true love shed abroad in our hearts by the Holy Ghost. We pray Thee that we may have joy and peace in believing. We pray Thee that we may be filled with the Holy Ghost, that the fruit of the Spirit may be manifest in us—love, joy, peace, longsuffering, gentleness, goodness, faith, meekness, temperance—so that men shall be obliged to take notice of us, that the Spirit that is within us is not the spirit of the world, but is a new spirit, even the Holy Spirit, and that we have been with Jesus.

Now, Father, we do not ask this of Thee as a mere form. We believe that Thou art. We believe that we have access to Thee by one Spirit, through Jesus Christ, and we come through that new and living way; and though we cannot use proper words to express our need when we pray to Thee, O forgive us what we are, and make us what we ought to be. It is not for much speaking that we ask Thee to hear us. We do not feel our need, neither know we how to ask for anything, as we ought; but what we ask Thee to do in the name of Jesus is to supply our need, to make us living members of the Lord Jesus Christ, producing very much fruit to Thy honour and glory, and to make us blessings to the land in which we live. We need Thy blessing, Father—Thy blessing and the light of Thy countenance,—that Thou teach the speaker to speak—that he speak by the power of the Holy Ghost, not in word only, but in demonstration of the Spirit and of power. O may the dead be awakened this night by the entrance of Thy word which giveth light, and may those who have it, have it more abundantly; and may it be evident that Thou canst take the weak things and the base things, and make them instruments in Thy hands, when it so pleaseth Thee, to do good. O may good be done, and no evil, and good above all we can ask or think. Accept us, not for our prayers, but because we ask it, most merciful Father in the name of Jesus Christ, our Lord and Saviour. Amen.

When preaching, North began quietly, almost diffident about taking on the holy task of preaching, but he quickly settled into his speaking and became more fluent. He read his text several times, slowly and solemnly, virtually emphasizing each word, gaining the attention of his congregation. His sermons were well prepared but were not written out or committed to memory. Since he was an itinerant preacher, some of his messages were frequently delivered, and his notes would be written on a blank page or in the margin of his Bible.

A minister once urged Brownlow to study more so that he would do more good. He told the minister that he spent three hours each morning studying the Bible and that, for the remainder of the day, he thought of divine truths as much as possible. The minister urged him to get a better outline, a more "connected form." Meekly he did so, and the next Sunday he preached to a full congregation. But after five minutes his chain of thought was broken and he stopped. There was a silence, and then he explained to his hearers that he had sought a new approach to preaching but that it had let him down. However, he had much to say to them about the Lord Jesus Christ, and soon he was powerfully presenting the gospel to them.

Another characteristic of North's preaching were his pithy statements. His sermons were peppered with striking aphorisms, hooks that hung on to the consciences of his hearers:

- The precise moment will come when you will have been five minutes in eternity.
- The devil has gained the whole world, and lost his own soul. Who would change places with him?
- Trying without praying, and praying without trying, both are a mockery. Let your motto be, Pray and try, pray and try.

- If a place is lukewarm, be sure the Christians in it are lukewarm. What do you do to prevent this lukewarmness? How much do you pray? How much do you labour? Lukewarm people make lukewarm ministers.

- "Ye cannot serve God and mammon." It is not said "do not," but "cannot."

- Those on the left hand are condemned for duties left undone and for negative religion.

- We speak of killing time: we expect a resurrection, but when will there be a resurrection of dead time?

- The smallest allowed sin is far more to be feared than the greatest evil that "we would not."

- If you are not sure whether a thing is wrong or not, and do it, it is wrong in you.

- As long as a man lets God alone, the devil will let him alone.

- Next to losing your soul, fear losing your convictions.

- A Christian is not afraid of death, but of sin; an unconverted man is not afraid of sin, but of death.

- Ignorance in religion won't save a man.

- God never says more than he means.

- There will be twenty knocks on visits of pleasure, even at a minister's door, for one of an anxious inquirer.

- Christians doubt because they are walking dubiously.

- Get your doctrine from the Bible. Get your example from Christ. A day will not pass after you have closed with Christ's promise, ere He will meet you with a counsel. Embrace both.

- Begin with sin pardoned and the law kept. What a beginning!

- No one can prevent your being saved but yourself. If you die the second death, you must be a suicide. God will say to you in the judgment, "Thou hast destroyed thyself."

- Every man's life is a prayer.

- Seek the wealthiest man in every city, and the holiest man in every city, and let their other circumstances be what they may, in every instance you will find that the holiest is the happiest.

- The sinner in Christ is his justification; Christ in the sinner is his sanctification. The two invariably go together.

- The whole question is not whether sin tempts or not, but whether it reigns or not.

- Are we speaking for Christ as we have opportunity? If not we are still in possession of a dumb devil.

- Godliness with contentment is great gain, but contentment without godliness is the greatest curse.

- If a man receives the Bible, he has to receive a great many things he can't understand, as well as a great many he does not like.

- Let the question of eternity have a monopoly in you. It is an intensely personal question, but instead of making you selfish, it will expand your heart. He who has never felt for his own soul cannot feel for another's.

- If Paul had not had the thorn in the flesh, we should not have had the blessed text, "My grace is sufficient for thee."

- God has no power to save sinners but by Christ: Christ is His Power.

- You say that you pray; but when you kneel down behind closed doors, will you believe that Jesus is actually at your side, desiring to bless you?

What we meet in Brownlow North is an evangelist and exhorter who focused on the unconverted (the openly godless and self-righteous) and on slumbering Christians. One proper lady heard him a few times and said, "He speaks as if people have never said their prayers or read the Bible." He could quote God's Word with much aptness and effect, and he preached most often on the chief doctrines of Scripture. They had conquered his mind, and he presented them vividly and with much originality to the intellect and conscience of men and women.

Chapter 6

Preaching in Edinburgh

When Brownlow North arrived in Edinburgh in early 1857, he went to the house of Alexander Moody-Stuart, the pastor of the large congregation of Free St. Luke's. The servant answering the doorbell was flustered upon opening the front door and meeting this imposing figure. He gave his name, but she, quite confused, knocked on the study door and told the Reverend Moody-Stuart that there was a Mr. Brown to see him. As Brownlow was ushered in, Moody-Stuart was still not clear about who this man named Brown might be. He thought, "He's a man of the world, but not a man of the world." Then North gave his correct name, and immediately everything fell into place. They conversed and prayed together, and Moody-Stuart was moved by North's reverence, earnestness, and tender spirit. For North, his host was a man with a fear of the living God, a brokenness of spirit, and faith in the gospel. Moody-Stuart found in North a man after his own heart. Their lives became knit together in the bonds of warm affection, and he asked North to preach for them on the next Lord's Day evening.

To get a seat in church when Brownlow was preaching, people would have to arrive at least an hour before the service was due to commence, and many were turned away disappointed. Early attendance and sitting in silence for an hour before the service was a requirement for all who came to the church, even for the gentry—that is, the hunting and fishing class of landowners who had been North's closest associates before his conversion. None denied the reality of the great change that had taken place in North. In his sermon he would refer to his conversion and to various incidents that had occurred, and then he would warn everyone of slighting the convicting work of the Holy Spirit in their lives. "Give yourself to Christ," he would exhort, "and take Christ instead." He would say "God is" so often that it could have been called his motto. He often challenged his hearers as to whether they believed in God or in their own hearts: "Unconverted people follow their own hearts. They do what their own hearts tell them, not the word of God. They read, 'Lay not up for yourselves treasures on earth' but their hearts tell them to take their ease; eat, drink and be merry. Now I want God's people to do just this, to put God's word where their own hearts used to be, and their hearts where God's word is. Believe God's word! Do what it bids you! Disbelieve your own heart. Don't follow your heart's teaching and suggestions."

After the first Sundays in Edinburgh, he often preached in Free St. Luke's in weeknight services and on the Lord's Day, always to packed congregations. He would stay in the manse, and during the mornings a succession of men and women concerned about their relationship with God would come to talk with him. One day a twenty-two-year-old man called to tell him of his conversion. He had been listening a few days earlier to Brownlow North preaching on Matthew 6:6, "But thou, when thou prayest, enter into thy closet, and when thou hast shut thy door, pray to thy Father which is in secret; and thy Father which seeth in secret shall reward thee openly," and he had come under such conviction that he headed home determined that he would give his heart and soul to God. But as he walked along the road, he came under a strong conviction that he should not delay until he had reached his home. It was too long, and so at that moment he stopped, knelt down on the cold pavement, and yielded all that he was to all that God is.

Brownlow North often felt that he had failed in his preaching. A close friend, Francis Brown Douglas, wrote down some of his recollections of Brownlow's preaching in Edinburgh:

> It was not always that what he thought his best ser-mons were his most successful ones. Many godly ministers have stated their experience to be the same. One evening he preached from the text, "Turn ye to the stronghold, ye prisoners of hope," dwelling on each expression. When he came home, he said he had never felt more unfit to preach than that Sabbath eve-ning; it was as if his thoughts were gone and his mind weak—there was no power at all in him; words would not come. Often he had more to say than he could get out, and was obliged to stop from exhaustion, but that night he stopped early, not because he was tired, but because he had nothing more to say. Yet he seldom had *so many inquirers coming to speak to him as after*

that address. One young woman, he told us, burst into tears and said, "O sir, when you said the devil was blinding our eyes and holding us down fast in chains, it went through me like an arrow; it was just my case."

On such an occasion Brownlow North read to us the following letter received that day: "Sir, excuse the liberty taken by a stranger in thus addressing you and trespassing on your precious time; but you love to do good to the souls of your fellow-creatures. You requested the prayers of a praying people: may I, who have no one to pray for me, request your special prayer on my behalf, that God for Christ's sake would enlighten my darkened soul, take from me the hard and stony heart, give me a new heart and right spirit, and loose the chains that bind me to Satan? While listening to your address, the most fearful thoughts took possession of my soul, which if clothed in words would make the most hardened shudder. O, pray, pray that I may be converted, sanctified, saved. I am an orphan, and almost alone, with none to whom I can tell my sorrow of heart, and must still remain a stranger even while making this urgent request."

Edinburgh bustled with the news of Brownlow North's preaching. He wrote with wonder to his beloved aunt, Miss Gordon, and vividly described his itinerations among all the good and great of Edinburgh:

My beloved auntie,

I really feel ashamed at not having written for so long, but indeed you would excuse me if you saw how I am pressed. I hardly know what to begin to tell you, but I do hope the Lord is with me. I have had to do with many awakened and anxious souls. May He own the work, and make the end to be true conversion of the heart to Him, for Jesus Christ's sake! Doors upon doors have been opened upon me, and the interest to hear seems on the increase still. Last Sabbath I was in Dr. Candlish's; Monday, Charles Brown's; Thursday, Moody-Stuart's; tomorrow, if God wills (and if He does, may He exceedingly bless), Haldane's old church at half-past two, and Moody-Stuart's at night; Friday, Dr. Brown's, the original U. P. On Sabbath, the 19th, by his own personal request, couched in language I should not like to repeat, at half-past two (his own usual service) I preach in Dr. Guthrie's Church. The wise, the mighty, the learned will all be there: may God be pleased to perfect His praise out of the mouth of me, a very babe in Christ, that am not worthy to be called a babe; but by the grace of God, I am what I am, and I hope by the will of God I am where I am. Oh what a glorious honour! May I just do so much, and no more than He chooses! Letters have come up from Thurso to Sir George Sinclair, asking him to get me to go over there for the herring-fishing time, when thousands are gathered, and he has earnestly pressed it on me, so that I think it seems a duty to go. Believe me, with much Christian love,

Your truly affectionate,
B. North

A newspaper reporter in March 1857 also described well his early days in Edinburgh:

Brownlow North, Esq., a connection of the great Lord North, and hitherto a careless "man about town," has been preaching in various Free Church and Baptist pulpits during the week. On Sunday evening he held forth in Dr. Candlish's church to one of the largest audiences it ever contained. He is a man apparently about forty years of age, as destitute of pulpit airs as when he was a leader of fashion and a keen hand for the turf: but in spite of his short shooting-coat, and the negligent tie, and the gold eye-glass dangling on the breast of his tightly-buttoned coat, there is tremendous energy and force in his preaching. There is something contagious in a man who is terribly in earnest. North begins his service with a low faltering voice; but before he has got half through the opening prayer, his breast begins to heave with a convulsive sobbing, his whole frame is agitated, and the tears stream over his cheeks. There is then no faltering. The words come quickly, and all the graces of a natural orator are developed. He becomes a great example of the truth that there is no teacher of elocution like the heart. When he implores his audience, with tears, to forget all about the messenger in the message; when he graphically sketches the position of the gay worldling, evidently picturing from experience, but scarcely ever alluding to his own past career; when he breaks out abruptly, in the middle of a sentence, with a radiant smile, and states the happy conviction that some souls are being saved; and when, with unaffected simplicity, he asks the prayers of the congregation on his own behalf, that he may be supported in the extraordinary position in which he finds himself, no unprejudiced spectator can doubt that he is a man in earnest, and that we may yet expect to hear great things of the work which he has begun. There is a significance in his appearance at this time which affects the future of the Church. As a spur to the regularly educated and regularly appointed ministers, and as a powerful living commentary on some of their most prevalent and fatal defects, Brownlow North seems destined to exercise a wide influence as a reformer.

Before he left Edinburgh he thought it wise to take out a life insurance in favor of his wife. One of the staff, filling in the forms, asked him if he knew of anything that might have shortened his life. "Oh yes," he replied, "I feel that I may not live for an hour." He had felt since his conversion that he did not have long to live. However, a medical examination judged him to be in good health and that he could live for twenty more years. He subsequently said to Moody-Stuart, "How many souls may I be the means of saving in that time!" In fact, by the providence of God, he did live for another twenty years.

Chapter 7

Recognition as an Authorized Evangelist

An evangelist is not self-appointed and does not lack accountability to a sending church. He is a member of a congregation and receives its counsels as his membership delights and motivates the church members. But he is also given enormous freedom by the church concerning his time, gifts, and labors. Brownlow North was the son of an English rector and had received theological training in an Anglican college. He spent his mature years in Scotland and believed and admired the Westminster Confession of Faith and the Free Church form of worship, psalm singing, and church government. He also believed strongly in the priesthood of all believers and that all Christians had a duty to proclaim to their neighbors the good news of salvation through Jesus Christ. In the margin of his Bible at Acts 8:1, where we read that the disciples "were all scattered abroad throughout the regions of Judaea and Samaria, except the apostles," and in verse 4, "They that were scattered abroad went every where preaching the Word," North wrote, "Surely this is in itself sufficient warrant for lay-preaching." Then, alongside similar verses in Acts 11:19–21, North wrote, "The success of all work for the Lord depends on this, the hand of the Lord being with us. Those preachers had no ordination from man. Because the hand of the Lord was with them, these lay-preachers turned many." But he was very concerned lest any should use his example to encourage people to believe that a stated ministry was unnecessary. He said, "I believe that next to his word and his Spirit, a minister taught by the Holy Ghost is the best gift God has to give to us."

After some years of his effective preaching, a strong desire began to rise in various quarters that Brownlow North should receive formal church recognition as an evangelist, and this took definite form within the Free Church, the denomination that from its separation from the state in 1843 (sixteen years earlier) had been most zealous in reaching Scotland with the gospel. Once North had become a professing Christian, its congregations welcomed him and opened their pulpits to his preaching.

In May 1859 the General Assembly of the Free Church, moderated by Principal Cunningham, met in Edinburgh and prepared and submitted an "overture" to the church that Brownlow North be recognized as an evangelist. Information concerning this intention was given to the church, and there seemed to be general acceptance. As the subject of North's acceptance was read to the assembly, one of Moody-Stuart's children smiled at some of the language used in reference to North, and the evangelist noticed the grin. North caught him afterward, teasing him, "Why, sir, are you laughing at me? Don't you know that I am now a probationer of the Free Church of Scotland!"

The overture stated that the assembly should formally welcome and sanction North in the labors of the gospel in which he had been involved during the past three years. This overture was signed by sixty-eight ministers and thirty-eight elders. Three professors were appointed to interview North as to the soundness of the doctrines he believed, and after meeting with him they told the assembly they unanimously recommended that it should welcome him as a friend of the Savior.

The motion was open to debate, and one of the first to speak was Professor Gibson, DD, a man whose conscientious jealousy for orthodoxy and soundness in the faith was proverbial. What would he say to this unusual recognition of gifts in a man not a member of the Free Church of Scotland or trained in their school? Dr. Gibson cleared his throat and addressed the assembly, stating that he had never, on any occasion, heard a more distinct, simple, and lucid statement of the doctrines of grace as those declared by Brownlow North: first, in relation to the condition of man as a sinner in the sight of God, dead in trespasses and sins, and as to the sovereignty of God in the election of grace; second, as to the method of a sinner's justification, solely and entirely through the imputed righteousness of the Lord Jesus Christ; and third, in reference to the perpetual obligation lying even on the sinner to obey the law of God as well as its binding and unchangeable nature required from every believer. The believer's duty, in gratitude and love to God, is to show forth God's law in his life and conduct. Nor had he ever heard a more clear statement of the work of the Holy Spirit in relation to the condition of man as a sinner, utterly unable and indisposed to anything good till renewed by the Spirit of God.

After a few similar words of warm advocacy from the most formidable leaders of the church, including professors at New College and the church's ruling elders, the motion to officially recognize Brownlow North was proposed and unanimously agreed to. He came forward to the table of the house amid loud and general applause. The moderator, Principal Cunningham, then addressed Mr. North in the name of the assembly. Cunningham's learning and devout love of the confession and the Scriptures, his mastery of theological controversies, and clear judgment made him the most suitable man for this happy task. This is what he said:

> Mr. North, I have great pleasure and heartfelt satis-faction in announcing to you that I have been called, by the unanimous decision of this House, to recog-nize and welcome you as a servant of Jesus Christ who has received unusual gifts for preaching the glad tidings of great joy, and whose work in this depart-ment the Lord has greatly honoured. The General Assembly has come to this decision, I believe, in full knowledge, and on deliberate consideration I concur heartily with the grounds on which this judgment has been adopted. I never could see the warrantable-ness of any Church of Christ venturing to lay down as a resolution that she would never see, and would not recognize, gifts for preaching or for the ministry, except in men who had gone through the whole of the ordinary curriculum. No Church has a right to lay down that rule. This Church has not laid down that rule, and I trust never will. The Church must lay

herself open to consider exceptional cases, to mark God's hand, and to make a fair use and application of what He has been doing. I believe, if we leave an opening for occasional exceptions, it will be of more importance in enabling us to maintain a high standard and full compliance with our strict regulations in regard to nineteen-twentieths of our students, than by attempting to carry out the same rule to the whole twenty-twentieths, and thereby running the risk of lowering the standard of the whole body, and losing, besides, the benefit of the exceptions. I have very great pleasure, Mr. North, in tendering you the right hand of fellowship, and in recognizing and welcoming you as a servant of the Lord Jesus Christ, and as highly honoured by your Master in your work. And perhaps you will allow me to say that your position is a somewhat peculiar one, that while you have eminent gifts, there are, of course, difficulties and temptations to which, in your position, you are exposed. I have no doubt you will feel that you stand deeply in need of wisdom and guidance and discretion; and I have no doubt you will feel that, amid all the encouragement you have had, you have still much cause to wait upon God, and walk humbly with Him.

Upon concluding his speech, the moderator gave Mr. North the right hand of fellowship, amid loud applause. This was also given by Sir Henry Moncrieff, Dr. Beith, Dr. Grierson, Dr. Wood, and others.

Brownlow North appeared deeply affected, speaking with difficulty at the outset of his remarks, and addressed the house as follows:

The Lord says, "How can ye believe, which receive
honour one of another, and seek to the honour that
cometh from God only?" Now, I think that at this
moment I have received an honour such as it is
impossible to exceed. For me to have been sitting
in this House, and listening to the language I have
been hearing, and to have been welcomed as I have
been welcomed, nothing can exceed the weight of
all these things, language cannot express that which
I feel put upon me at this moment. And I do earnestly request the prayers of this Assembly, that what
the Moderator so kindly and affectionately put me in
mind that I require, may be granted to me. One of
my own prayers has been, from almost the first day
that I prayed at all, that I might receive marvelous
grace, and marvelous grace to bear the marvelous
grace. To find myself where I am at this moment, I
can only say I trust and believe it is the Lord's doing,
but it is marvelous in our eyes. Dr. Candlish told me
yesterday, that I would probably be asked to say a few
words to-day and that it would be on the subject of
the state of religion in Scotland. I have had an opportunity during the last three years, of seeing much of
the religious state of the country; and I have come to
this conclusion, that although we are by God's grace
gathering many prisoners out of the chains of sin and
Satan, still it is but a single one of a city, and two of
a family, and that the whole world is no better now
than in the days of the apostle, when he said, it was
lying in wickedness. Now, dear friends, by the help
of God's Spirit how much might not you, who are
now before me, effect in leavening this putrid mass
of iniquity? I believe there are *four special things* for

which God is very angry with the land, and for which His Holy Spirit is so little among us.

1. First the neglect of united prayer—the appointed means of bringing down the Holy Spirit. I say it, because I believe it, that the Scotch, with all their morality so-called, and their outward decency, respectability, and love of preaching, are not a praying people. Sirs, is not this the truth? The neglect of prayer proves, to my mind, that there is a large amount of *practical infidelity*. If people believed that there was a real, existing, personal God, they would ask Him for what they wanted, and they would get what they asked. But they do not ask, because they do not believe or expect to receive. Why do I say this? Because I want to get Christians to remember that, though preaching is one of the great means appointed by God for the conversion of sinners, yet, unless God give the increase, Paul may plant and Apollos may water in vain; and God says He will be inquired of. O ministers! Excuse me— you gave me this chance of speaking—urge upon your people to come to the prayer-meeting. O Christians! Go more to prayer-meetings than you do. And when you go to the prayer-meeting, try and realize more that there is use in prayer.

2. Secondly, I do not believe that there is a more effective system in Christendom for the promotion of true religion than the Presbyterian system…if it were carried out. But the machinery is not working. Look at the mass of elders there are in the Presbyterian Church. But what are these elders doing *as a body*? Blessed be God, there are many holy, self-denying godly men, who seek not their own things, but the things which are Jesus Christ's, and who go into the lanes and alleys of the cities, and pray, and speak, and try to lead people to God. But do the elders, as a body, do that? I believe there are elders—it is possible there may be such in this very Assembly—who know that God, who searcheth their hearts, sees that from week to week, and from month to month, they never make a single attempt to do anything for the glory of Jesus Christ, and such must give an account to God at the last day.

3. *The third point is that men are entering the ministry without a call or gift from God.* I have seldom or never heard touched upon, because, perhaps, men hardly know how to alter it, but I believe it ties at the very heart's core of the irreligion of the land; and it is this, in the church of England, and in all the Presbyterian churches of Scotland, and I doubt not, in all other bodies, men are brought up from childhood to say that they are going into the church. Men are put to college and educated for the church, and men in England are brought before their bishops, and in Scotland before their presbyteries, and without any fear of being struck dead for committing the blasphemy against the Holy Ghost, they swear in my church, they state in yours, that they believe they are called by the Holy Ghost to the ministry, and that they enter it out of a desire to promote the salvation of the souls of their fellow-creatures *and they know when they say it they tell a lie.* I say there are multitudes of instances of this: even in this Assembly there may be those who know that they have been guilty of this fearful

sin, for even among the twelve apostles there was a
Judas, even in this Assembly there may be those who
have even now no reason to believe that they have
been born again of the Spirit, and who are nothing
but hireling shepherds. Oh, if there be, I implore you
to conceive [of] your position! If it was a dreadful
thing for the rich man to think of the entrance of his
five brethren into hell, knowing how their reproaches
would increase his torments, what will the entrance of
your congregations into hell be to you? How will you
bear their reproaches? Think of it! The day of judgment will come, and if you know in your hearts that
you are not yet converted, and are not really labouring
for souls, as those called of God to labour, ah, follow
the advice that Peter gave to Simon Magus; confess
your sins to God, pray for pardon and the Holy Spirit,
and for the baptism of that fire which can yet enable
you to awake the dead around you; and then, instead
of being lost for ever, you may yet appear before God
in glory with many children which may still be given
you. Brethren, bear with me. I do not presume upon
my position: but if I lose this opportunity of speaking, no man can tell if I will ever have the like again. I
asked God this morning to bless me, and to give me a
word that should be blessed to you.

*4. Lastly, the very best amongst us are exceedingly guilty
in neglecting the apostolic injunction to be instant "out
of season."* How solemn is the introduction to the
command, *"I charge thee therefore before God, and
the Lord Jesus Christ, who shall judge the quick and
the dead at His appearing."* "I charge thee"—what? *"Be
instant in season, out of season."*

Now, we can all speak when we are expected in the pulpit, in the prayer-meeting, or at the family altar, but are we faithful out of season? I feel convinced if the godly minister would prayerfully commence a system of individual, faithful, personal dealing with his people in their own houses, speaking as one who was in earnest, and beseeching men not to rest in a mere form of godliness, but to be content with nothing short of God's Spirit witnessing with their spirit that they were born again, that he would very soon see of the fruit of his labour, and have reason to bless God and take courage. We need more *out-of-season work*, more talking to people apart in private as to the state of their souls.

Mr. North concluded, amid applause, by thanking the assembly for the honor done him and by expressing his hope that he might never give them any reason to regret it. The assembly then prayed that God's blessing might rest on his labors.

Chapter 8

Correspondence

Soon, throughout that great age of letter writing, correspondents were writing to Brownlow North, and he spent much time during the remainder of his life in answering his mail. The following are samples of some of the letters he received.

A Letter from a Sailor

H.M.S…April 5th, 1860

My dear Sir,

I take the pleasure of writing to thank you for the great blessing you have been the means of bringing upon a most hardened and wicked sinner. You may remember coming to preach one Sunday on board the ship. Your prayer was heard that day. The Lord sent your words home to the heart of one of the greatest sinners who was listening to you, and who thought he had been so vilely used that there was no truth in religion or in the Bible; one who reviled God's truth, and argued against it, and many times said man had no pre-eminence above a beast, and brought the Bible to prove it, and in fact had almost become an infidel. But you stopped me: I heard you say you had been guilty of almost every crime, you thought, except murder; so I thought, "That's a plain speaking man. I'll just pay attention to him," not thinking to do much good by it; but when you asked if we ever thought upon God, it went like a shot through me. I had forgotten Him altogether.

Family distress in fifty-four, when I sailed home in the Frigate…had driven God out of my thoughts, and the devil took the advantage, and goaded me on to drink, and ran me into all sorts of evil. Your coming on board that day just saved my soul from his snare; but I have had to struggle hard, as you told us. I prayed to the Lord Jesus to assist me, and He has done so, and has beaten him; and I am happy to inform you the good Spirit is master within, and shall never more be drowned by an evil one. And now instead of reviling God's truth, I adore it, and read it earnestly, and pray while reading for the Lord to open my eyes to see the hid treasures therein contained; and I think He grants my prayer; and instead of not being able to think of Him a minute without some worldly thought coming in, I think of Him long and often. I found all you said true. I was eating husks all my life till now. I never was so happy before. I often think of you, sir, and pray the Lord to prosper all your efforts, and may His blessing ever attend you for the blessing you have brought on me. My heart is full.

From yours ever thankful,
A. B.

P.S. There is a prayer-meeting on board this ship every night. It was held in a cabin, but they are obliged to go

into the stoke-room, the cabin was not large enough
Mr. Palmer (the Lieutenant) attends with the men.

A Letter from a Student

Aberdeen, March 2nd, 1863

My dear Sir,

I regret much that I have been deprived of a
personal interview with you, though I have been
privileged to hear you every time you have preached
in Aberdeen. I therefore take the liberty of sending
you this note to tell you that I have never repented
the choice I made some seven years ago, when, in
Albion Street Chapel, you pointed me to a personal
Saviour. Very often, to my shame and confusion, have
I proved unfaithful and treacherous; but so great has
been His love to me, that He has not cast me off, but
has again and again gone after His lost sheep in the
wilderness, folding me in His bosom, and speaking
words of cheer and comfort. I have been frequently
in the depths, often in the hot furnace, and of late in
the wilderness; but wherever I am, there He is; and
in the very wilderness He has given me songs, vine-
yards, choice dainties. Oh His love, His forbearance,
His tender mercies! Would I could praise Him more,
and were moulded into His glorious image! In a few
months I expect, D.V., to be licensed, but I shrink
back from the work when I think of its awful nature
and responsibility. Oh! try sometimes and remind
Jesus of me, that I may be an able minister of the
New Testament, one dead to self and to the opin-
ion of the world. The Lord has had much to do with
me, a proud, stubborn, wayward child; but He sees

my heart, and knows that it is my earnest desire and prayer that I may sit at His feet and learn of Him!

Yours very truly,

J. H. C.

A Letter from a Woman in England

March 3rd, 1862

My dear Sir,

I desire to express my warm gratitude, first to God, and then to you, who were the means to me of enlightening and quickening in the way of grace. I attended every one of your public weekday addresses during my visit to Edinburgh, and was led by them to regard religion as a more real, personal thing than before. I have known these things as long as I can remember, with the head, perfectly, but my heart had become so accustomed to them, that I took them all as a matter of course, and thought for years that I was a Christian. On hearing you, however, I doubted it, and was very happy for some weeks, going about to establish my own righteousness, trying to make myself better before I came to Christ and miserable because I could not "feel" good, nor sorry, nor anything that I ought to feel; and this remained up to the middle of your last address, Thursday, Feb. 27th, on Romans 10:1–4. Then I saw by God's Spirit, that I must not consult my "feelings" any longer, but give up all my own righteousness, the good as well as the bad: and I was the more ready to do this, having proved that my righteousness was as filthy rags; and that I must take Christ's righteousness as my own, a free gift imputed to me. And I have been joyful in Him ever since. Now I know what faith means, and why it is "precious faith." I could not before understand those words, "Believe on the Lord Jesus Christ," for I did not know what to believe about Him. But now all things are new: the Bible has depths I never saw before; Jesus Christ is to me "wisdom, and righteousness, and sanctification, and redemption." I cannot praise Him enough for revealing Himself to me; and I am most grateful to you, dear sir, as having been the means of showing me this new life. I thank you especially for having shown it so clearly in the Bible; for now, if any doubts arise, I can turn at once to those passages, Romans 3:20–24 and 10:1–4, which brought me, through the grace of God, life and salvation.

I remain, with deep gratitude, yours sincerely,

M. J. F.

Then there are the letters he wrote to his correspondents.

A Letter to a Young Christian Woman

Newcastle-on-Tyne, Thursday, May 13th, 1858

Your last letter has been forwarded to me to this place, and I received it and your former one with much pleasure. May you seek and obtain strength from the Lord Jesus Christ to perform the covenant you have entered into; for remember His own words, "Without me ye can do nothing" and let your present feelings and confidences be what they may, be sure of this, that unless you abide in Him, and His words abide in you, you will perish at the last, like the stony-ground hearers, who, when tribulation ariseth for the word's sake, are offended and fall away. I write not these things to trouble you, but as my beloved child I warn you; for you have a terrible conflict before you, and have need of the whole armour of God on the right hand and the left. Your enemies are exactly described, and not one jot or tittle exaggerated, in Eph. 6:12. Therefore, as a good soldier of Jesus Christ, buckle on what God has provided for you; and never counting yourself to have attained, but ever coveting earnestly more and more of Christ's true riches, that you may lavish them as fast as you receive them on those who have need, go boldly forward, strong in the Lord and in the power of His might, looking unto Jesus, who, for the joy set before Him, endured the cross, despising the shame. Remember, looking unto Jesus is the great safety. Perpetually endeavour to realize His real personal presence and existence, and then what this real Person has done and suffered for you, and so you will catch something of His Spirit, and will be willing to do or suffer for Him. Do not take your Christianity from the example of those around you, however excellent they may be, but study the life of Jesus, how He acted and how He spoke, and serve to speak and act as He did. Above all, be constant in private prayer. Beware of the first beginnings of shortening private prayer. Be you hot, cold, or lukewarm, still pray; and going as you are to God, ask Him for Christ's sake to make you what you should be. May the Lord make you a burning and shining light, remembering that humility is the first of the Christian graces, and may He give you to win many souls by your chaste conversation and meek and quiet spirit (see 1 Peter 3:3&4). I have written more than I intended when I commenced. May God bless it to you. And ever remember there is no truth in us, in our hearts; that the only truth is in the Word of God. He that trusteth in his heart is a fool, but he that believeth in the Lord Jesus Christ shall be saved, saved not only from the punishment of sin, but from the power of it. So when your heart says one thing, and the Lord another, believe Him whom you have now, in the presence of God, of men, of angels, of devils, taken for better, for worse, to love, honour, and obey, as your Lord and your God.

A Letter to a Man Objecting to the Christian Faith

March 24th, 1859

Sir,

You may easily imagine I have little time for letter-writing. I return your letter, that you may, by having it by you, better understand my answer. Until you are willing to condescend and humble yourself to every one who is likely to be better instructed than yourself in divine things you cannot enter into the kingdom of heaven. Secondly, man is not to ask, but believe. The natural man has no reason that can help him, no spiritual discernment. Read (first going on your knees, and asking in Christ's name for God's Spirit to lead you) the first three chapters of 1st Corinthians, beginning at the eighteenth verse of the first chapter; read two or three times carefully, and may you be taught to cease from your own wisdom, and to seek the "Spirit which is of God, that you may know the things which are freely given to you of God" (2:1&2). It is written, "The just shall live by faith"; and, God helping me, I have made up my mind to stand or fall with Jesus Christ. If He is the truth, I am saved; if He is the truth, the man who leans to his own understanding is damned! Awful position!

No safety except Christ. Christ tells me in the fifth of John, verses 19, 23, "that whatsoever things the Father doeth, the same doeth the Son, that all men should honour the Son, even as they honour the Father." I do so; therefore, if I do wrong, I plead His own word; I can't do more. The Bible is full of that which can only be received by faith. I never try to reconcile. It is certain damnation if we refuse to receive what we cannot reconcile. See the irreconcilable yet heavenly thing, "And no man hath ascended up to heaven but He that came down from heaven, even the Son of Man which is in heaven" (John 3:12&13).

Your second question I answer as Paul did the blasphemer's in Romans 9:18, 19. Because God chose it, and it will not lessen the agony of the penalty, that through the countless ages of eternity you continue asking, why? why? Let it be sufficient for you—It is so. Shall not the Judge of all the earth do right? And though the answer to your question is not revealed, it is revealed that if you will do His will, you shall know of the doctrine, whether Christ spoke of Himself, or whether it be of God. Crucify therefore your own pride and carnal inclinations, as one who feels eternity to be at stake. I would wrestle with you in the name of Jesus for the Holy Spirit to lead you. Diligently shape your life as He directs you. May He bless you! I send you the 5th, 6th, 7th, 8th verses of the third of Proverbs: "Trust in the Lord with all thine heart, and lean not unto thine own understanding. In all thy way acknowledge Him, and He shall direct thy paths. Be not wise in thine own eyes: fear the Lord, and depart from evil. It shall be health to thy navel, and marrow to thy bones." Take the counsel there contained, and the promise in the last verse shall be fulfilled in you.

Yours with much interest,
Brownlow North

A Woman Who Had Benefited by His Preaching

Strathleven, Dumbartion, December 30th, 1858

My dear Friend,

I must send you a line to say how heartily I congratulate you on the news you are able to give me about A. May the Lord bless him and keep him, and He most surely will if he will only believe God's Word, and not his own lying heart and feelings. Nothing can prevent God's doing the mightiest of works in and for a poor sinner that goes to Him, but unbelief. You pray, and the answer too often is, "I can do no mighty work because of your unbelief." The command is, "Whatever you ask, believe that you receive." It would be good for us all if we would look at God more as "the God of truth," and whenever anything is suggested to our belief, to ask ourselves, "Can this that I feel or think be true if God is true?" and if it cannot, then make God truth, and your own heart the liar. All sin has its origin in making the devil the God of truth, and God the Father of lies. This is the cause why the careless man continues in sin, and the anxious man in unbelief. They believe the statement of their own spirit, and disbelieve the words of God's spirit. Give my kindest Christian love to your dear husband, and ask him to read the enclosed, a copy of which I purpose to send to every minister in Scotland.

B. N.

A Newspaper Reporter

W. T. McAuslane was on the staff of the *Glasgow Morning Journal* newspaper when he went to report on one of Brownlow North's meetings in the Queen's Rooms in Glasgow. He transcribed the service well, but he did something better: he paid heed to what he was hearing, and he was converted that night. Some months later he wrote to Brownlow North concerning how he might get assurance of salvation, and this is the evangelist's reply:

Dear Sir,

I have received your most interesting letter, and regret that I have not found time to answer it sooner. I have now great pleasure in answering the questions you propose to me, as far as my own light and knowledge enable me. May God the Holy Spirit, for Jesus Christ's Sake, teach us both.

1. You are to believe God's word without any other warrant whatever, simply because it is God's word; but doing so will necessarily produce peace and joy. Feelings are to flow out of faith, not faith out of feelings. If you really desire the pardon of God, and His favour, if you believe you have it, because He says He will give it you if you ask it for Christ's sake, you must be glad.

2. Yes, if what God says and what you feel cannot both be true, let God be true, and your own heart the liar.

3. The feelings which faith should produce are love, joy, peace, a hatred of sin, and a desire after holiness. No doubt they will vary, because our faith varies, and all in us is variable; but we should ever remember that He never varies, but is always the same to

us (Mal. 3:6). Satan's great object is to get us not to trust God, but God's command is, "Trust in Him at all times" (Ps. 72:8).

4. When you can see Christ, you may look at your sins, your frames, or anything else you please; but when in darkness or doubt, or fancying yourself without Christ, you must look at nothing but Him. You must leave every other object of contemplation, and gaze at what He is, what He says, and what He has done. For He says, "I am the Beginning," "the Alpha," "the Foundation"; and we must begin with and also build all on Him.

May God make it clear to you what you desire to understand. Endeavour to obey the injunction contained in the first eleven verses of 2 Peter 1, and try and DO righteousness, whether you like it or not. It is never said like it, but do it. And recollect God's definition of love in 1 Corinthians 13:6, John 14:21, "He that hath my commandments, and keepeth them, he it is that loveth me." With much interest,

Yours sincerely,
Brownlow North

This letter gave the reporter much comfort, but this was temporarily terminated by a minister who told him that 1 John 1:9, "If we confess our sins, [God] is faithful and just to forgive us our sins," was a promise for Christians and that a sinner was not entitled to appropriate it. W. T. McAuslane again wrote to Mr. North in his difficulty, and the evangelist's reply gave him comfort and peace:

My Dear Sir,

In regard to your friend's statement, that 1 John 1:9 was written for Christians, I answer, that a Christian is a man who believes what God says in the gospel of His Son, and that a man becomes a Christian the moment he believes. Scripture cannot contradict itself, and no confession of sin is considered as such by God, where there is not an intention to resist it and forsake it but the man who goes to God by Jesus Christ, and asks for pardon for His sake, and does not believe he gets it, makes God a liar, as much as does the man who says he has no sin. See 1 John 1:10, in connection with the previous verse. If we confess our sins, and say we do not know whether He has forgiven us or not, when He says His faithfulness and justice are pledged for our pardon, we make Him a liar. I believe faith to be a thing of degrees, and that a person may be in a state of salvation, and yet be very hopeless and desponding. Such a state, however, is quite foreign to the intention of the gospel. There is a great difference between faith and fellowship, or communion. This is promised to a certain line of conduct pursued after faith. Believe me, with much interest,

Yours in Jesus,
Brownlow North

Brownlow North also wrote a tract that was sent to the ministers of Scotland. It was widespread, and one still reads it in different magazines and columns addressed to young Christians.

Six Short Rules for Young Christians

I. Never neglect daily private prayer; and when you pray, remember that God is present, and that He hears your prayers. (Heb. 11:6)

II. Never neglect daily private Bible-reading; and when you read, remember that God is speaking to you, and that you are to believe and act upon what He says. I believe all backsliding begins with the neglect of these two rules. (John 5:39)

III. Never let a day pass without trying to do something for Jesus. Every night reflect on what Jesus has done for you, and then ask yourself, What am I doing for Him? (Matt. 5:13–16)

IV. If ever you are in doubt as to a thing being right or wrong, go to your room, and kneel down and ask God's blessing upon it (Col. 3:7). If you cannot do this, it is wrong. (Rom. 16:23)

V. Never take your Christianity from Christians, or argue that because such and such people do so and so, that therefore you may (2 Cor. 10:12). You are to ask yourself, how would Christ act in my place? Then strive to follow Him. (John 10:27)

VI. Never believe what you feel, if it contradicts God's Word. Ask yourself, Can what I feel be true, if God's Word is true? and if both cannot be true, believe God, and make your own heart the liar. (Rom. 3:4; 1 John 5:10&11)

Chapter 9

Theology

An interesting conversation took place between two leading Christian personalities in nineteenth-century Scotland: Dr. John "Rabbi" Duncan, the Old Testament professor in New College, and Brownlow North. They were sitting in the home of Dr. Moody-Stuart when Rabbi Duncan said to him, "Mr. North, you are an untrained theologian." "Oh, very untrained," replied the evangelist. "You mistake me," said Rabbi Duncan: "My emphasis was not on the word 'untrained' but on the word 'theologian.'" Rabbi Duncan spoke of Brownlow North as a "born theologian" and would go to his meetings as often as he could, listening to him with the humility of a little child. Dr. Henry Cook, the great Irish preacher, told a number of his fellow ministers that Brownlow North was one of the best theologians they could hear.

His grasp of biblical theology is one reason that crowds of people continued to flock to his meetings and listen quietly to his sermons twenty years after his conversion. He was a great preacher of Christian doctrine. He could say to his discerning congregations, "'Free from sin' by justification; 'servants to God' by sanctification, and the two cannot be separated." His style was not at all flowery. Rather, he was terse and plain, quite unadorned: "Jesus' blood! Nothing more is needed. Nothing less will do. Feed on Jesus' body and blood." K. Moody-Stuart heard him often and described his sermons as clear, powerful, earnest expositions of major truths. He spoke solemnly and forcibly with moving application. He seized the leading aspects of every doctrine, majoring in the important revealed truths so that they came with fresh impetus and moved his congregations to adore and wonder. North would say, "When once God gives a sinner to Christ, or Christ to a sinner, God never changes his mind."

Nineteen-year-old Charles Haddon Spurgeon became the minister of New Park Street Chapel in London in 1854, the year of Brownlow North's conversion. What remarkable events, taking place within months of one another! Nothing is impossible with God. In one lecture to his students, Spurgeon said the following words, which were exactly the conviction of Brownlow North: "Do not believe that when you go into revival meetings or special evangelistic services, you are to leave out the doctrines of the Gospel, but then you ought to proclaim the doctrines of grace more rather than less. Teach gospel doctrines clearly, affectionately, simply, and plainly, especially those truths that have a present, practical bearing upon man's condition and God's grace."

He Preached on the Living God

He pressed on his hearers the fact of God's existence as a burning reality. That truth could come to a congregation with a terrific force, and he would follow it by pressing on his hearers its momentous consequences. The God and Father of our Lord Jesus Christ—our Creator, the God who gives us our purpose in life, the God whom we have sinned against, our coming Judge, the God with whom we all have to do—He lives! He is the God of the Bible, of the patriarchs, the prophets, the apostles. He would frequently say "God is" with great solemnity. He would often quote Psalm 14 regarding the fool who says in his heart that there is no God. The fool says that not because of a lack of evidence for God's existence but because of his moral defiance. North regarded atheism as the sin of sins, and he challenged his congregations on this point. Most of his hearers would assent to God's existence, but in fact they were denying it because there was no outworking or practical consequences in their lives of sincere submission to God, no hunger to know Him better, and no obedience to Him as their good Master. Brownlow North traversed Scotland, filling churches with solemnized hearers who had this fact constantly pressed on them—"God is!"—the existence of a personal God who had revealed Himself in the Bible and in Jesus Christ. If the Bible were true, then the consequence for all his hearers was that they are all lost men going to destruction. Other evangelists preached the way of salvation and the cross of Christ as Brownlow North did. He was no different from them, save in this: he preached the divine existence as no other evangelist of the nineteenth century.

Preaching in Elgin in November 1862, he quoted the verse, "He that cometh to God must believe that he is" (Heb. 11:6). That is the first verse in the whole Bible that he wanted to get into their hearts. He said, "If I could give to every one in this large congregation a practical belief that GOD is, the God and Father of our Lord Jesus Christ, that God really sees us, and hears us, and will save us if we come to him, then I would be glad to shut this Bible and go home and bless God for it to all eternity, for I believe that this is the grain of mustard seed which will grow into the great tree in the end."

He preached this in a manner that adorned that truth. He himself had a sense of the divine presence in the words he used, the way he opened up the livingness of God, and the solemn way he looked at the congregation—his awe, his gestures, his whole bearing—so that many in the congregation who had come out of curiosity felt, "Surely God is in this place, and I knew it not." Even those who did not feel the impact of God's presence did feel that North believed it with all his heart and that he was the spokesman of a real, living, divine power that had the speaker in His grip. He delighted in preaching Christ.

He Constantly Asserted the Truth of Scripture

When he was first converted, his hopes of life and salvation were found in the Bible. He had put his hand on the Scriptures, having read these words of Romans 3:22, "the righteousness of God which is by faith of Jesus Christ unto all and upon all them that believe," and said, "If that Scripture is true, I am a saved man." Twenty years later, in the final days of his life, he spoke to an officer in the army and said to him, "You are young, in good health, and with the prospect of rising in the army; I am dying; but if the Bible is true, and I know it is, I would not change places with you for the whole world."

He viewed the rise of higher criticism of the Bible in Scotland with alarm. Once when preaching to a large gathering in Edinburgh, he told his audience that he had recently led a Bible class for a popular minister and had been grieved by the diversity of views of Scripture among the young men attending it. For North, the doctrine of inspiration was a matter of life or death to the believer. He would exhort his hearers, "You have got Bibles, read them! You cannot understand them unless the Holy Spirit teach you, therefore pray for the Holy Spirit." He said, "The distinguishing mark between God's people and others is this, that God's people prove everything by the light of God's word."

The order of his teaching was (1) God is, (2) God is a person, (3) God is present, and (4) God has spoken, or rather God speaks in the Bible. The Word is instinct with life, and it comes to the hearer or reader as if newly uttered by the mouth of God. North would quote the opening verse of Psalm 28: "Be not silent to me: lest, if thou be silent to me, I become like them that go down into the pit." It was essential that his parting words when counseling the troubled Christian or the seeker would be "Go home and read your Bible." One of his favorite verses was, "Heaven and earth shall pass away, but my words shall not pass away" (Matt. 24:35).

He Declared the Immortality of the Soul

Up to this point the cults who denied the doctrine of the soul's immortality had made little impact on the United

Kingdom, but there was growing hostility to the Bible's teaching on the eternal punishment of the rebel and the Christ rejecter. The first tract North wrote, which was often reprinted, was titled "You Are Immortal." It opens with the words, "Reader, you are an immortal being. You have been born, and you will have to leave this world, but you can never cease to exist. You must live for ever. It is of no avail to you that you are so debased by sin that you would wish to be like the brutes that perish. I know that all this may seem very dreamy and unreal to you, but it is nevertheless true." In his preaching North would rivet his audience, saying, "I can tell you to the minute how long your life is to be; it is to be as long as the life of God." As people listened, he told them, "You could no more go out of existence than could God."

The truth of Jesus's words on the eternity of hell is very awesome and mysterious, but it was also a constant in Christ's ministry and in the ministry of His apostles. It is to be handled with humble submission and the greatest tenderness, keeping to the confines of what the Holy Spirit has written in His statements and to the emotional framework in which the Savior Himself spoke. The Lord Jesus said, "These shall go away into everlasting punishment: but the righteous into life eternal" (Matt. 25:46). Alongside those words, Brownlow North had written in his Bible, "The duration of the punishment of the wicked and the life of the righteous are equal." When he was asked about the unforgivable sin, he said, "If you are willing to give up sin and go to Christ, then you cannot have committed this sin…. The man who has a good thought left is not left by God."

He amplified this when speaking to the students in Edinburgh University, saying to them that no man has committed the unpardonable sin who has a good thought in his heart and the least desire to go to God—even if he is a hundred years old and his sins are very many. Then he urged them, "Today if you will hear his voice, harden not your heart."

He Preached the Sovereignty of God

Brownlow North believed all the great tenets of the Westminster Confession of Faith. He said, "Paul clearly teaches the doctrines of divine election and also human responsibility. I cannot reconcile them. Neither could Paul, but there they are, and the election is God's, and responsibility is ours." He certainly preached that man is responsible and answers to his sovereign God. He would say, "No one can prevent your being saved but yourself. If you perish, it must be your own act and deed. If you die the second death, you must be a suicide. God will say to you in the judgment, 'You have destroyed yourself.'" He would quote these words, "Lazarus is dead.... Nevertheless let us go unto him" (John 11:14, 15), and then look at the congregation and say, "No matter, dead and stinking, Jesus will come to us, and can raise us up, and he will if we ask him." These convictions had come to him from his daily praying and studying of Scripture since the time he first believed.

Regarding the extent of the atonement, he believed that Christ loved the church and gave Himself for it. His Savior was the Jesus who had come to save His people from their sin. North believed that Christ's blood was sufficient for all men but was efficient only for those who believe. Because he had such reverence for the redeeming power of Christ's sacrifice, he did not preach a universal redemption. How could the Son of God die in order to save those who were going to be condemned to hell? He did not and could not limit the power of the blood of Christ, but he limited the purpose of His dying love to saving that innumerable company whom His Father had given to Him to seek and save.

Yet how Brownlow North declared the freest offer of salvation to all who were hearing the Word of God being preached to them! In writing of North's evangelism, Moody-Stuart stated,

> His Calvinism did not in any way hamper him in declaring the freest offer of salvation to all, and pressing its instant acceptance upon every sinner to whom the offer came. The salvation he preached was as free as the sunlight, as authoritatively pressed on every gospel hearer as the august command of God can press it, and as urgent as it can be made by the exactest meaning of the word NOW. Sufficient for all, suitable for all, offered in gift to all, pressed upon the immediate acceptance of all by the invitation, the entreaty, and the command of God, such was his gospel— and can anything be more free, more full, and more unfettered? No doubt he also insisted on a natural aversion to it, inability to understand it, and incapacity to receive it. But over against this he held out an offer and gift of the Spirit as free as the offer and gift of the Saviour, thoroughly to overcome that aversion, to remove the blindness of the understanding and the alienation of the affections. Human language cannot

express a salvation more overflowingly full and more unconditionally free: God offering His Spirit to lost and helpless sinners as freely and unconditionally as He offers His Son.

Brownlow North, in speaking of the seriousness and responsibility of believing on the Lord Christ, would remind his congregations that Jesus was said to have marveled only twice: at the faith of the centurion and at the unbelief of the people in His own city.

Of course, Brownlow believed that man's fallen state consisted also in a determined opposition of his will to the will of God—not a free will but a will serving sin that can be removed only by the Holy Spirit. Our will must be brought into conformity with the Lord's. Salvation is never forced on an unwilling recipient, but each gospel hearer is called on to exercise his will in an act of choice, to choose for himself this Lord to be his God. But the alteration in our wills to choose what is entirely contrary to their natural disposition is wrought by the will of God working powerfully in them, transforming them, as it is said, "Thy people shall be willing in the day of thy power" (Ps. 110:3).

Very powerfully did Mr. North press on all his hearers their duty to willingly take Christ. One of his most widely blessed discourses was a spiritualized exposition of Genesis 24:58: "Wilt thou go with this man? And she said, I will go." Soul after soul in different parts of the country were brought to the point of decision and of closing with Christ through that sermon, in which he throws the whole responsibility of the choice on the hearer yet states unambiguously at the very outset that "by the power of the Holy Ghost" his hearers or readers may answer as Rebekah did. On John 6:37 he noted, "If we are really going to Jesus, this verse assures us of two most comfortable things: one, that Jesus will in no wise, for no reason whatever, cast us out. The other, that we must be among the number given Him, or we would not have gone to Him." And again, "If Christ rejects a coming sinner, He must also reject a drawing Father." Again, on John 8:43–44, "Ye cannot hear my word…. The lusts of your father ye will do," the "will" explains the "cannot." You cannot, because your will is in opposition. To reject the gospel message is a greater sin, and will bring on us sorer punishment than the grossest immorality.

The success of North's labors can be attributed to a number of factors: his compassion for the lost, his earnest longing that they be saved through Christ alone, and his magnifying the grace of God before them. He challenged those who said that they did not believe in sudden conversion by giving seventeen examples of this in the book of Acts. He said, "Jesus did not ask Martha did she understand this, but if she believed this. And Martha at once replied, 'Yes, Lord.' Because though she did not understand it, she believed it, because Christ said it." Brownlow said, "No matter what instrument is used to bring us to Jesus, no matter what the disease may be, if we do but go to Jesus, he will in no wise cast us out."

The reason for the stability of those professing faith under his preaching can also be attributed to North's insistence that their trust be in the person and work of the Son of God alone. Man cannot be saved by any moral goodness that he imagines he has. He cannot be saved by any experience or strong feelings he has known. Was it his experience that died for him? Were his strong feelings raised from the dead on the third day for him? That was the Lord Christ. Let them have Him and let them cling to Him alone for eternal life. He cried to his hearers, "Begin with sin pardoned and the law kept. What a beginning!" Brownlow North also hemmed them in to the Spirit, writing in the margins of his Bibles these words: "No man can ever know anything of God or of the things of God, unless they are revealed to him by God's Spirit. Pray for the Spirit. He is promised to all who ask. If Paul had not received the Spirit of God, he could have known nothing. There is no real wisdom or knowledge outside of God and of Christ."

Chapter 10

Ministry in the Irish Revival of 1859

Scotland and Ireland are very close geographically. On a clear day the mountains of Antrim in Ulster can be clearly seen from the coast of Ayrshire. The two nations are also ethnically united; both are Celtic countries, as is Wales. Scottish Presbyterianism was brought to Ireland centuries ago, where it has maintained a confessional identity. These ties of race and churchmanship provided a sympathy and kinship that made it very easy for Brownlow North to accept an invitation to preach in Ireland, and he was further encouraged to travel there when he heard that a powerful religious awakening was taking place. He had a strong desire to see what was happening there, as did many of his friends in the ministry who had sailed to Ireland to witness events firsthand. So when the moderator of the Irish Presbyterian Church, John Johnstone, wrote to Brownlow, giving him details of the awakening and inviting him to address the General Assembly meeting in Dublin in 1859, he readily accepted.

What follows is a brief summary of the Irish revival according to Rev. Gareth Burke, currently the minister of the Stranmillis, Belfast, a congregation of the Evangelical Presbyterian Church of Northern Ireland.

THE BEGINNING OF THE 1859 REVIVAL IN ULSTER

In the spring of 1856, an English lady by the name of Mrs. Colville came to Ballymena from Gateshead because she had "time and money to spend for God." She began a program of house to house visitation with a view to winning souls for Christ. In November she returned to England in low spirits thinking that God had not acknowledged her labors, and feeling that her work had been unfruitful. However, she was wrong. Just a few days before she left, she had visited a certain Miss Brown who lived in Mill Street, Ballymena. On calling at this house, she had found two other ladies present as well as a young man called James McQuilkin. McQuilkin came from the parish of Connor about five miles from Ballymena, and he worked in a linen warehouse in the town. Miss Brown and her companions were involved in a discussion on the subjects of predestination and free will. When she entered the house, the others asked Mrs. Colville whether or not she was a Calvinist. She did not answer this question directly but rather spoke to the little group about the importance of seeking a personal interest in the Savior and the need of the new birth. What she had to say concerning the Savior left a profound impression spiritually upon James McQuilkin, and a short time afterward he came to a saving knowledge of Christ. An unusual, unknown, earnest Christian lady was used by God in the conversion of James McQuilkin who was to become one of the most significant figures in the 1859 revival in Ulster.

James McQuilkin worked in Ballymena, but he returned home to Kells every weekend. Prior to his conversion he was known in the village as the man who reared fighting cocks. Now, however, his outlook on life had changed. He came under the influence of Rev. John Moore, the minister of Connor Presbyterian Church, who encouraged him to gather some of his converted friends together and to commence a Sabbath School at Tanneybrake near the village of Connor. McQuilkin and his three friends—Jeremiah McNeilly, John Wallace, and Robert Carlisle—felt their own inadequacies and inexperience in the work and so in the autumn of 1857, they took an old schoolhouse near Kells where they could meet for prayer and seek God's blessing upon the work of the Sabbath School which they had recently established.

During the next few months, some other believers joined with the new converts for prayer and, in a short time, in December 1857, they were encouraged by the conversion of a young man for whom they had been praying. Over the next few months, several other people in the district came to saving faith in Christ, and soon conversions were taking place nearly every week. At the spring communion in Connor Church, a special sense of God's presence was enjoyed by those present, and throughout the rest of 1858, conversions were taking place throughout the parish of Connor. By the end of that year, some fifty met regularly for prayer at the Old Schoolhouse prayer meeting, women not joining with them but having a separate prayer meeting of their own.

On December 9, 1858, Samuel Campbell came to know Christ in a personal, living relationship through the influence and prayers of the Connor prayer meeting. Mr. Campbell worked in Kells but belonged to Ahoghill. He desired to share the good news of salvation with the rest of his family in Ahoghill and encouraged the other members of the Connor prayer meeting to pray for him as he made several journeys across to Ahoghill with the purpose of witnessing to his loved ones. His brother and sister, in response to his witnessing, sought the Savior, but his brother John remained hardened and uninterested. Campbell persisted in his witnessing and one day, on visiting Ahoghill, he boldly shared Christ with his brother whom he found out in the fields participating in a shooting match. "I have a message for you from the Lord Jesus," he said. John Campbell immediately came under conviction of sin and there in the fields his body began to tremble. With some difficulty he reached the family home where for some weeks he remained in agony of soul before obtaining an assurance of sins forgiven.

Rev. Frederick Buick of Trinity Church, Ahoghill, was greatly encouraged by what the Lord had done for the Campbell family. Recognizing the contribution that the Connor converts had made to the conversion of the Campbells, he decided to hold a meeting in Ahoghill at which a number of the new converts from Connor would speak about their spiritual experiences. The meeting was arranged for February 22, 1859, in the Ballymontena Schoolhouse.

However, so many people turned up that it was decided to walk the short distance to Trinity Church. This meeting had a profound spiritual impact upon the Ahoghill district, and many people began to pray earnestly that revival would come to their area.

On March 14, 1859, at the thanksgiving service at the close of the spring communion in First Presbyterian Church, Ahoghill, there was a significant outpouring of God's Spirit, and many came to a saving faith in Christ. The minister of First Presbyterian Church was Rev. David Adams who had prayed much for revival among his people since coming to the congregation in 1841. In 1858 a large new building had been erected capable of seating 1200 people. However, on the night of March 14, 1859, about three thousand people were present at the service which was conducted by Mr. Adams. During the service one of the Connor converts, Mr. James Bankhead, rose to pray. Interestingly, Bankhead also tried to address the gathering, declaring that a revelation had been committed to him and that he spoke by the command of a power superior to any ministerial authority! Mr. Adams, the minister, was less than happy with the way things were developing and, being particularly concerned that, amidst the crowding and commotion, the galleries would not carry the weight of the people, he called upon them to clear the building. Outside, in the village square, James Bankhead and other converts addressed the crowd from the steps of a house. Although the streets were muddy and it was pouring with rain, people listened for hours, with many falling down in the street and crying unto the Lord for mercy.

This marvelous work of God's Spirit—the work of revival—was beginning to spread throughout North Antrim. It is difficult for us living in the day of the internet and the mobile phone to imagine how slow communications were in 1859, and it is almost breathtaking for us to realize that the awakening which had begun in Connor in 1858 and had spread to Ahoghill in 1859 was still largely unknown in Ballymena, the major town in the county. But that was all about to change. This movement of God's Spirit was destined to affect not just a small corner of North Antrim, but very soon Ballymena and beyond would witness remarkable scenes—scenes of amazing spiritual blessing which still stir us in our own souls today.

When Brownlow North finally visited Ireland, he was accompanied by James Balfour of Edinburgh. They sailed from Greenock on a fine summer evening and stopped at a newsagent near the ship. On the counter, alongside copies of the Christian magazine *Revival*, sat a stack of tawdry magazines. Brownlow North looked at this incongruous juxtaposition and said to James, "What two books to be together!" The newsagent spoke up, "You are talking about something of which you know nothing." "How so?" said Brownlow. "You never read these books," he replied. "Have you read this magazine?" he asked the evangelist, pointing to the smutty magazine. "Indeed I have," said Brownlow. "I read it for many years. It is very clever, but very wicked. I am a changed man since I would read that book." The newsagent was silenced and then said defensively, "I know what best will sell." "Ah yes," said the evangelist, "if you are living only for this world. But remember you are immortal." Before he left the shop, he gave the newsagent a tract he had written titled "You Are Immortal."

The two men paced the deck as they sailed across to Ireland that summer evening, and upon arrival North immediately began preaching, night and day, in many towns. When he preached in the Victoria Market in Londonderry on a Sunday, almost five thousand people gathered to hear him. He spoke on Proverbs 8:1: "Doth not wisdom cry? and understanding put forth her voice?" He asked,

> How do we get to God? Jesus is the way to God. Through the rent veil of the flesh of Jesus we approach God. Man's wisdom only led him to dishonor God and destroy himself. I was once staying in a house amongst the high and noble, when a scoffer said aloud, "The instinct of the brute is higher than the reason of man." I was angry when I heard him say that, but later I reflected that the brute had an instinct that God gave it, but man had not reason as God had given it. If you are following your own wisdom, what hope do you have of escaping hell, even if you gained the whole world, unless the Bible is a lie? What is the great conflict between God and man? It is whether man would believe his own heart or believe the wisdom of God. If you really believed that Christ's yoke is easy, then you would take it this very moment. Wisdom in Proverbs 8 is the Son of God. He is calling the simple and foolish to turn at once from their folly and to fear God and hate sin. To love God is to keep his commandments. It is by faith in Christ that you are saved and not by your own feelings. The proof that you have received the Holy Spirit is not some sensation but your new power over

sin, for sin is your great enemy. There is one great gospel commandment, "Believe on the Lord Jesus Christ!" When my own spirits are low, I often rely on the words, *"Trust in the Lord at all times."* You must always abide in Christ. An unhealthy looking branch while it remains in the tree can become strong and vigorous. Christ's love to the branch abiding in him is like the Father's to his own Son.

But in the evening, to the same number he preached his great sermon on Genesis 24:58: "Wilt thou go with this man? And she said, I will go." The verse had struck him three years earlier in Inverness. He never stopped preaching on it, and in 1867 he published it as a twelve-chapter book titled *Yes or No?* It is the most accessible account of his preaching. Hear his urgency:

> How long have you to live? You say you do not know. Let me tell you. Your life is co-eternal with God. You have to live as long as God lives. It is true your life is not to be passed in this world. Your life in this world may be over any moment, *"then whose shall those things be that thou hast provided?"* Your life in this world bears a less proportion to the life that is before you than does the millionth part of a grain of sand to a million worlds crushed into powder. But he who had power to place you here, and who gives no account of his actions to any, has revealed to you that it is his intention to place you in another world—a world as real and actual as the one you now inhabit—with this difference that whereas this one is temporal and passing away, so that to which you are hastening is unchangeable and eternal, *This*

*corruptible must put on incorruption, and this mor-
tal must put on immorality.* And you, whoever you
are, have to spend an eternity in a world of misery,
or a world of glory. Whether it be misery or glory
depends upon what you live for here. And can you
be said to have done any real good to yourself, if you
have made no provision for eternity, but only gained
the things of this world?

In this revival there was a physical phenomenon of
convicted sinners fainting and falling to the floor. It happened in Brownlow North's meetings, although he never
encouraged it. He made little attempt to explain these
actions. When asked about it, he would say, "Either they
are of the devil, or of man, or of God. They cannot be of the
devil, for he never makes men anxious about their souls,
or desirous of fleeing to God. They cannot be of man, for
he cannot do it if he would—if he could, then he oftener
would. Then this must be of God." The problem with this
explanation is the identification of falling to the ground in
a faint with true conviction of sin. Time and testing would
later indicate that some who had prostrated themselves had
not been spiritually convicted of their sin. North put no
confidence in this physical reaction as any final evidence
that God had been reconciled to people who had fainted.
Did they have Jesus Christ as their prophet, priest, and
king? That was his ultimate concern.

Having preached fifty times, many of which were to
congregations of more than a thousand people, Brownlow
North left Ireland on August 26. At his last open-air service,
it was calculated that between twelve and twenty thousand

people were present. He exalted the truthfulness of Scripture and refused to countenance reliance on mere feelings. He encouraged his hearers to rely wholly on Jesus Christ, and as a result many sought his counsel and hundreds were confirmed in their faith. It was impossible to estimate the number of those awakened by his preaching. North himself was refreshed by what he had seen of the wonderful work of grace in the land, and the cry in Ulster was, "When will he come back to us again?" He had not been home a day before a minister named George Steen wrote a letter telling him of the influence of his ministry in Ireland:

> God has greatly blessed the word you addressed to us. A number of souls have been converted, and a still greater number are blessing God that their faith in Jesus and his written word has been greatly confirmed.... I held eleven public meetings last week, taking the dinner hour, from one till two o'clock, and in the evening from seven until nine, and everywhere I went we had crowded meetings. Our people began last Lord's Day at half-past seven in the morning, pleading for the outpouring of God's Spirit upon the Sabbath school. And with the exception of their hours for breakfast, dinner, and tea, the whole day was spent in devotional exercises up to the hour of ten at night. They would not, could not part; it was a blessed season of the sweetest communion.
>
> There is hardly a meeting I hold in the country but I hear some sinner telling of mercy received, or some child of God speaking of great enlargement of heart through your services, and I invariably beg of them to prove their love to you by commending you and yours to the oversight of the Saviour.... One

peculiarity of the present moment is the coming of *poor simpletons* to Jesus. John, a creature who gathered rags, has been for eight weeks one of the most devout worshippers of the Lord, and although he confesses that he is a poor sinner, yet his hope is so fixed in Jesus that he lives in prayer and praise. In one meeting house a prayer meeting was being held on a Monday evening. After the divine service was over, a Roman Catholic simpleton, who had walked there for two miles, came forward. He was very tall and clothed in a woman's dress. He earnestly requested that the minister and people would pray "that he might be washed in Christ's precious blood." Singular sight, and still more singular request!

George Steen acknowledged the presence of bodily manifestations such as fainting. People were later ashamed of some of the things they had said, but even Peter on the Mount of Transfiguration had spoken foolishly. The Reverend Steen closed the letter to Brownlow North by saying, "Oh, I wish all our ministers would give over all their wise solutions of these strange visitations, and work for God! What we don't know we'll know hereafter. Meantime, we know Jesus is the physician for all, and his blood the balm for all."

Chapter 11

First Visit to London in 1859

London was ready for the arrival of Brownlow North. His conversion and preaching had been well known to evangelical Christians, but now he had accrued an extra dimension. He was the most well-known preacher to have ministered in the Irish revival. His first meeting in London was a full Exeter Hall, which Spurgeon had regularly used. So that there would be no particular denomination claiming Brownlow North as theirs, the first meeting was held on December 20 under the auspices of the YMCA. It was well received, and Brownlow remained in London until the spring of 1860. An older evangelical Baptist named Baptist Noel invited him to preach at his pulpit, and soon he was preaching at the Presbyterian church on Sundays and during the week, always to full chapels.

North's presence in London and connections with the archbishop of Canterbury and the prime minister suggested to a number of Christians that he would be the very suitable choice for reaching the nobility and upper classes, especially during the height of the season in 1860. One such meeting was arranged, and the organizers were so pleased that they arranged for a series of weekly meetings to be held, each one to growing numbers in an atmosphere of serious attention.

I once spoke to Dr. Lloyd-Jones about his early impact on Port Talbot, suggesting to him that the sudden fame surrounding his leaving medicine in London had drawn many people to come to hear him. He rejected my suggestion totally: "It did me no good at all," he said. "They came with curiosity to see me. They weren't listening to what I was saying. There were no conversions for six months, but then they began to listen to what I was saying." So it was for North in London. There developed a riveted attention rather than curiosity and "idlers seeking a new distraction." Many displayed an intense heart-longing for higher, eternal things. Conventional reserve about guilt and how a man might know God personally was overcome. After the last of these meetings for the nobility came to an end, a special meeting was announced for anxious inquirers, and almost six hundred people attended that gathering.

Spurgeon had transformed evangelism in London by holding meetings in theaters and great halls in various parts of the metropolis. Within a couple of years of Spurgeon's outreach in the Surrey Music Hall, three separate committees had been formed, buildings were hired, speakers were invited, and money was raised to pay the costs so that the poor of London (who paid no pew rent to guarantee them a place in churches on Sundays) could hear the gospel "without money and without price."

Brownlow North preached in St. James's Hall and in several of the theatres in West and South London, giving his testimony and laying on his hearers the necessity of taking their stand in following Christ and preparing to meet God. "I am more anxious for your salvation than you are for your own," he would tell them. But the next step was, in a way, even more revolutionary. Were there not at hand large Christian meeting places? What of St. Paul's Cathedral, Westminster Abbey, and other such buildings throughout England? Soon those who had been shocked at music halls resounding with hymn singing and the solemn hearing of the Word were again happily disturbed to discover that national edifices, which had become almost religious museums, were being filled for gospel services, the singing of great hymns, and the resounding entreaties of coming to Christ and finding rest in Him.

Brownlow North was one of the preachers at St. James's Hall when three sisters went one evening to hear another speaker. A friend told them that they should come on the following Sunday when "a gentleman will preach whom if they once heard him they would never forget him." The three girls went along to hear Brownlow North preach his unforgettable message on "Wilt thou go with this man?" They came under fearful conviction of their sin, and one of them subsequently said, "I only remember that I felt under his preaching that there really was a heaven and a hell, and that Mr. North believed in both."

That sister married a Christian man named Frank White, who heard North as often as he could. His discerning comments about his ministry are worth considering. The evangelist had a peculiar freshness that made his whole ministry quite startling and attractive. He told people of the wrath to come in language that, although strong, was not more so than was consistent with what a faithful herald of God may proclaim. He had a deep sense of the reality of the penal judgment of God. As Frank White noted,

Another striking feature of his ministry was that he addressed the consciences of his hearers; he spoke of sin in plain terms; he insisted upon repentance toward God as equally evidence of entrance into the kingdom of God as faith in the Lord Jesus. But what, perhaps more than anything else, made his ministry so valuable and should move us to ask the Lord to raise up more like him, was the fact that he gave no uncertain sound about the imputed righteousness of Christ. I shall never forget him once preaching on this, taking for his text Romans chapter 10 and verse 4, "Christ is the end of the law for righteousness to everyone that believeth." He remarked, "Men, in their endeavour to work out a righteousness of their own by keeping the law, generally begin here (and with this he pointed to the elbow of his left arm), and try to work up to their fingertips, but they make no real progress. Only after repeated failures to and falls in seeking to keep the law do some favoured sinners see that Jesus Christ is the end of the attempt to get a righteousness by keeping the law. Only in our Lord's perfect obedience alone can we be justified."

Chapter 12

Visits to Colleges and Universities

Like any evangelist, Brownlow North saw the potential for
the church's future vitality and growth in the lives of young
men who had given themselves to God's service. He was
a forerunner of those meetings to which only men are
invited. Some who were encouraged to attend would not
have gone to regular evangelistic services. Moody-Stuart
could think back to attending such gatherings twenty years
earlier, and what characterized them in his experience was
a deep solemnity and awe hanging over the vast crowds
of young men who attended them. Every winter during
the years surrounding the 1859 revival there were unforgettable meetings for men held in St. Luke's Free Church
in Edinburgh as well as similar meetings in the great cities of England. The YMCA in meetings all over the United
Kingdom invited Brownlow North to preach sermon series
such as his "Wilt Thou Go with This Man?" Official letters
of invitation would be sent from the local secretary, and
quite often there would be a postscript headed by the word
Private, with the secretary writing something like, "We
have never met, but it might encourage you to know that

you were the means of bringing me to a saving knowledge of Christ in such and such a place ten years or so ago."

Students' meetings were held during the 1859 revival, and Brownlow North addressed some in Glasgow. They were attended by ministerial candidates for the pulpits and manses of the Church of Scotland, and he was particularly concerned about an unconverted ministry: "You are occupying a pulpit, week by week, and yet you are a stranger to the saving grace of God! You are not preaching his gospel. You are failing to bring light and blessing to your congregations. You are unable to help those who come to your meetings asking the question, 'What must I do to be saved?' While unsaved yourself you cannot be a blessing to them. Oh, beware of being cumberers of the ground! Are you entering the ministry solely for the social position it brings you, and the comfortable stipend?"

Rather than shouting at the congregation, these words were spoken with deep pathos and yearning, his voice tremulous with concern, tears rolling down his cheeks. Brownlow was deeply earnest that these theological students should know conversion. He was very solemn in exhorting them not to think of the ministry without the assurance that the Lord had wrought a saving work in their lives. To convert others to become disciples of Christ, it was essential that they themselves knew that they had already become His disciples. These meetings resulted in a remarkable movement in the University of Glasgow and also in Aberdeen under the ministry of Reginald Radcliffe of Liverpool. One consequence of this was a student prayer meeting held weekly in the 1859–1860 academic year. The men of Aberdeen also wrote a letter to the students in Edinburgh, which was printed and circulated among the whole college. It exhorted them to come to the Lamb of God, gather together for prayer meetings, regularly read the Scriptures, maintain their life with God, and bear witness to their fellow students. Most of the students had never prayed in public or spoken to other students about following Christ. They were quite fearful about how they should respond. They knew who were the Christians on the university faculty, and they asked Professor Campbell Winton of the Department of Civil Law if they could use his classroom on Saturday mornings, and he was delighted to agree with their request. Occasionally they approached a professor to speak to them.

On the first Saturday of March in 1862, Brownlow North was invited to speak to them, and another Christian member of staff had been approached and asked if they could hold the meeting in his classroom. He readily agreed, and the students put up notices in the college that Brownlow North was coming. Some were immediately torn down. There was opposition in the air. Here, at the seat of learning, the out-of-date message of the three Rs was being preached to the students: man ruined by sin, redeemed by the sacrifice of the Son of God, and regenerated by the Holy Spirit. What was this crude theology but an attack on the fruits of the Enlightenment itself?

A senate meeting of the university was to be held. The Christian students wrote to the university principal, Sir David Brewster, asking him to confirm the use of the room for the visit of Brownlow North. Although he was most sympathetic with the request, he told the evangelicals that he had only a casting vote, and a number of professors had approached him and told him very plainly that they opposed Brownlow North's speaking in the university. The senate debate was hot, long, and acrimonious, and the supporters of Brownlow's visit were forced to back down. Permission to hold the meeting was withdrawn. However, lecturers at the neighboring Royal College of Surgeons under the leadership of the outstanding Sir James Simpson heard of the opposition and immediately responded by putting their largest classroom at their disposal.

The opposition had given North's visit the best possible publicity, and the classroom was filled to its utmost capacity, with many having to stand outside the building. A speedy decision was taken to move down the street to a neighboring church, Free Roxborough, and the students crowded in and listened with quiet attention. The meeting began with a dozen Christian staff members from the university getting up, walking to the front, climbing the pulpit steps, and standing on the platform. Many Free Church ministers and elders joined them there, all standing like a guard of honor around Brownlow North. Professor Sir James Simpson introduced himself and explained how they came to be assembled in a church building and not the university on that day. Facing a thousand students, James Simpson introduced Brownlow North, saying,

> Why have you asked Mr. Brownlow North to address you? I believe the simple answer to that question is this, that many of you are aware that by God's grace and under God's hand, Mr. North has been the happy

instrument of arousing the attention of many to the important matter of religion; and you students must ever remember that of all the truths you have to consider, that is the most tremendous, because it bears not only on the concerns of this life, but on your joy or misery, your salvation or your ruin through eternity.

Mr. North has been blessed in an extraordinary manner in expounding the doctrine of our redemption by Jesus Christ, a doctrine which is perhaps rejected by many because it is so essentially simple. Let me add that Mr. North, as a lay-preacher, has perhaps some advantages over more professional preachers, for we do know that a kind of conventional language is sometimes employed by the regular clergy which perhaps injures the efficacy of their preaching. Let me read to you some words of Dr. Thomas Chalmers.

Then Simpson opened Chalmers's *Lectures on Divinity* and read his quotation from his friend Robert Hall, in which he claimed that the majority of evangelical preachers did not know how to lay down the gospel so that a man of plain and ordinary understanding could know how to receive it. Having introduced Brownlow North and stood in solidarity with him and his message, he called on the Rev. Dr. Thomas Guthrie to lead in prayer.

Brownlow North came to the pulpit and humbly spoke of God's dealings with him. Then he announced his text, Psalm 119:9: "Wherewithal shall a young man cleanse his way? by taking heed thereto according to thy word." There was a serious listening, with one student commenting, "He made me feel as if I were moving among unseen realities."

Another student later wrote, "I remember the seat in which I sat in the top gallery; I have forgotten text, sermon, everything but one expression, one I have often heard from him since, but which had not struck me before. He said these words, 'If God's word says one thing, and your head says another, call your heart a liar, and believe God.'"

Chapter 13

Methods in Evangelism

The Earl of Aberdeen was a great supporter of Brownlow North, arranging meetings for him in the little country churches around that city as well as organizing major services in the largest buildings in Aberdeen itself. He wrote, "As a public speaker, and as an example of pulpit eloquence, I know of none who surpasses Brownlow North. His voice and delivery are truly admirable, and the affectionate earnestness of his manner is irresistibly winning, while his practical knowledge of the subject and his powers of lively and clear illustration give to his words a force and weight which it would be difficult to overestimate." It was the Word of God that achieved the lasting good in Brownlow's entire ministry.

Yet the earl was concerned over two matters in Brownlow North's life, the first being that the evangelist was doing too much, taking too many meetings, and traveling too frequently. He wrote to Mrs. North, pleading with her to "use your influence and get him to spare himself for the sake of others as well as himself, and to take care of his health which he is so ready to neglect, and to prevent his wearing himself out in doing good to others." How much Mrs. North was able to curtail Brownlow's preaching is a moot point.

The second matter is rather mysterious. The earl's wife recounts that her husband "saw very clearly, and deeply regretted, some weaknesses in the evangelist's character which he thought did some injury to greater usefulness, and he did not hesitate to tell Brownlow North his concerns, but he did this so gently and tenderly that the evangelist, far from taking his faithfulness amiss, expressed his gratitude to him for speaking so plainly, and their friendship continued unaltered to the last." What those perceived faults were, we have no way of knowing.

But what were the distinctives of his meetings? The services were very plain. There is no record of special music or soloists ever being employed, and in Scotland people typically sang metrical psalms unaccompanied by instruments. After worship would come the reading of God's Word and a prayer led by a local pastor, after which the evangelist stood and preached. There were also significant differences from many of our meetings today.

First, the congregations were largely God-fearing citizens who filled every seat in the churches and halls. For example, each winter North preached to nearly 1,500 people in Free St. Luke's for many days, and the congregation contained an overwhelming majority of prayerful, serious-minded, discerning church members who had been giving themselves to earnest intercession that the Lord would bless His Word that evening and throughout the week, so that the people they had brought along—especially their own children—should be saved. The singing was holy, heartfelt, and very moving, and the congregation held the preacher in great affection. Many of them had sat under the searching ministry of the pastor of Free St. Luke's, the Reverend Moody-Stuart, for years, so the corporate testimony in North's gatherings came from these sensible and kindly people who were evidently in complete harmony with the contents of North's preaching as well as the spirit of urgency with which he preached.

Second, there were meetings after the sermons for those who had been seriously affected by them. At the close of the service, the congregation quietly and swiftly filed out, leaving the building empty, and then immediately the doors were reopened and hundreds who had remained waiting outside returned into the church and sat down, listening intently while Brownlow North exhorted them concerning the nature of closing with the Lord Jesus and living the Christian life. Many of these wanted to talk with him further in person; in fact, on one Saturday after he had preached for a week in Free St. Luke's, seventy anxious inquirers had made appointments to meet the evangelist. One was a boy of sixteen who had been brought to the meetings the night before by his aunt. He was greatly affected by what the evangelist said:

> The language, which was unmistakably that of conviction, was rendered more forceful by his manner of delivery, not only his voice, but every feature of his face displayed the urgency of his message. I had never doubted that there were such places as heaven and hell, yet I'd never so far believed in them so as to let their existence affect my life. At the conclusion

of his address I believed that hell existed, and I further believed that I was in danger of going there. My aunt asked if I should like to see Mr. North and it was arranged that I should see him the following day.

Brownlow North had told an old friend who was the manager of a home for women that he would come that Saturday to speak to the people living there. When a coach was sent to pick him up, it returned empty with a note of apology saying that he was sorry to disappoint his friends but he dare not abandon these convicted men and women who wanted to meet him. He later explained that God seemed to have used one moment in the sermon to awaken a number of hearers: "It was something I said about 'grace and peace' that broke them down. I had said, 'You are all wanting peace. But you won't humble yourselves to take grace. You remember that grace and peace are linked together like the steam engine on the track pulling the train. They are attached to one another. The engine must go first and then the train follows. You must have grace, the forgiveness of sin, or you can never have true peace.'"

After a while the shy sixteen-year-old boy had opportunity to meet him. The teenager had been struck by North's seriousness and solemnity during his sermon, but on this occasion he was touched by North's kindness and concern for his soul: "He seemed more anxious about it than I was myself. He spent some little time in explaining my difficulties, then we kneeled down and he prayed with me, displaying at every stage such a sense of the preciousness of my soul that it was quite new and striking to me. The apprehension of the dangers and temptations he foresaw I should be exposed to seemed to affect him much. When we rose from our knees, he hugged me tenderly, and I left him thanking God for this opportunity he had given me."

Finally, the evangelist showed great skill in personal dealings with the men and women who came to see him "both in season and out of season." He did not hurry people into the kingdom of God. He did not give assurance to seeking people that they were now in Christ. He did not try to do the work of the Holy Spirit for Him. He would not take God's grand prerogatives from Him. No man can share the honor of bestowing a free justification. Salvation is of the Lord and through the Lord, not by us. North's chief concern was to show to these inquirers the imputed righteousness of Christ—who of God was made unto us wisdom, righteousness, sanctification, and redemption—and then beseech his hearers to receive the Lord.

He tirelessly counseled and advised the people who came to see him. A young woman told him she was concerned that if she became a follower of Christ, she could no longer go to dances. He looked at her and kindly said to her, "Rather ask whether going to a dance is the way in which I can most profitably spend my time? That is the question for the servants of the Lord." There was another man who had been affected by rationalism and was offended by Brownlow North's direct speech. Subsequently the man could not bear to remain in the same room as the evangelist. Brownlow noticed this, and it would have been the easiest thing to accept that providence and ignore the man, but he could not. He approached one of the members of this man's family who was a Christian and was liked by the old man. Brownlow gave to that person one of his books and asked that it might be passed on to the recalcitrant fellow. That was done in a sweet and kindly way, and he began to read it, which changed his whole tone toward Brownlow North. He even would smile at him and was open to reconsidering his message. When Brownlow stayed in lodgings, he always told the landlord or landlady that he would be worshiping at a certain time and that any of the people working in the hotel or any other guests could join him in his room for that occasion. Those invitations seem always to have been accepted, and in one seaside resort the landlady's two daughters were blessed by their attendance at his family worship.

In North's evangelism, he did not have an "inquiry room" to which people were invited at the close of the sermon. He did not number the alleged converts from the rest of the congregation. He would be approached by numbers of people who wanted spiritual help. He would ask permission from the family with whom he was staying if these inquirers could come to the house at various specified times during the day. Then, at the end of the week of meetings, he would pass all their names on to the householder or the leader of the meetings. He would earnestly exhort these people in private (and generally all the congregation in his preaching) to attend the regular ministry of the pastors in that place and to be present in Bible classes. Prayer meetings knew an increase in attendance after his visits. Of course, there were those who proved to be stony ground hearers, but a large proportion turned out well. There was a strange reluctance to attend the Lord's Supper for the first time in the weeks following North's visit. Many who had shown evidences of conviction of their sin and their need hung back. They were afraid to make a spurious profession of faith and so simply attended all the means of grace, public and private, but the following year they had gained more assurance that it was well between their souls and God, and they applied to the church session for membership. Most of these remained earnest members of the congregation, active and consistent workers, for the rest of their lives.

Chapter 14

Seven of His Striking Converts

The Earl of Aberdeen often attended Brownlow North's meetings, and after one visit he wrote to the wife of the evangelist to express his appreciation of her husband's visit: "I am sure that my family and I have great cause to be grateful for the good he has done us. We are most anxious that you should use your influence and get him to spare himself for the sake of others as well as his own, and to take care of his health which he is so ready to neglect, and to prevent wearing himself out in doing good to others." The Earl also described the manner in which Brownlow North preached, which became such a force in the conversion of many. "As a public speaker, and as an example of pulpit eloquence, I know of none who surpass him. His voice and delivery are truly admirable, and the affectionate earnestness of his manner is irresistibly winning, while his practical knowledge of the subject and powers of lively and clear illustration give to his words a force and weight which it would be difficult to over-estimate." Let us consider seven of the converts that such a life and ministry produced.

Mary Ann Whyte from Inverness

Mary Ann Whyte came from the Scottish Highlands. Her father was a schoolteacher in the county of Inverness, and she had witnessed the death of her mother. She had been raised in a Christian home, and her acquaintance with death and her own uncertain health helped her to think seriously of the Lord of eternity. When the evangelist visited Inverness, she went with eagerness to hear him and came to assurance of salvation under his ministry that day. This is what she recorded as a teenager shortly before her death:

> I can tell you the time and the place when and where Christ manifested his love to me and caused me to love him with an everlasting love. It was on the evening on which I heard Brownlow North in Inverness. He preached from Genesis 24:58 on "*Wilt thou go with this man*?" I thought when Brownlow North was opening up the character of the Lord Jesus and showing us his matchless love to sinners that my heart too was correspondingly opening up. At one point he called out with the voice of God, "Here! Here! The Lord of heaven! The wonder of angels! The delight of saints! The desire of nations! He is here and now offering himself freely to you all for time and eternity. O will you take him? Take him! Take him! This may be the last offer you may have of him. Will you let him go? O don't!" I thought my soul was one flame of love for him. I would not…I could not…I did not let him go! I was aware that those around me were noticing my state, but I could not contain myself. I was overcome with love, with love that constrained me to love him, and since that time until now—and I believe for all eternity—I can think of none but him-

self. I put my hand on my heart and tell you that his
love is written here. He will soon grant me my desire,
and that is this—where he is there I may also be.

When asked if she was sure that she loved Christ, she
replied vigorously, "I am sure of that. Yes! He has made me
sure of it. As sure as I'm able to say it. Yes, surer than my
words because He has written it on my heart. Oh love of
heaven! Who can but love Thee? Art Thou not altogether
lovely?" At the end of her life she experienced a natural fear
of death but recovered from that phobia, saying, "Oh I see
it now. My own dear Jesus has the keys of death and hell, in
order to give me an easy passage through death, and He has
locked the cowardly enemy into hell. Alas that I should forget my Key!" One of her family members asked, "On what
are you venturing as you depart? On the peace and confidence God has given you?" Mary Ann smiled, "On nothing
but Christ…. On none but Christ. Feelings are sweet, but
trusting in them would be like fixing the anchor inside the
ship instead of in the rock." Then she added, "Tell Brownlow
North of my hopes and that I shall soon see him in heaven."

A Woman in Andrew Bonar's Congregation

Andrew Bonar was the biographer of his notable friend
Robert Murray M'Cheyne. He recorded an account of the
conversion of a woman in his congregation at Finnieston
Free Church. She had been well taught under his preaching and then awakened to her great need of salvation. She
eventually called at the house where Brownlow North was
staying and sat near him, covering her face with her hand
and not saying a word. He waited, expecting her to break

the silence, but the silence went on, tears running down her cheeks. Brownlow North tried to draw out some response, saying, "I suppose you are anxious…. I guess you have come to speak with me because you are anxious?" Not a word. Finally he said to her gently, "You know that I can be of no use to you if I don't know your state of mind. Tell me something of what you feel." No response at all. He waited there and looked at her, her face buried in her hands. There was another long silence, then there came the following exchange: "I need not try to speak to you unless you speak to me. I will have to let you go away, but at least answer me this question, Do you believe there is a God?" When he had pressed this question, her hand fell from her face and she said, "Sir, if I did not believe there was a God I would not be anxious about my soul." "Ah, now I understand you," Brownlow North said. "You're troubled because you know you have to have dealings with God, the God who is holy and a just God. Let me speak to you about him." Then the evangelist reminded her in his own way of what God had done for all who believe in Christ, that He had accepted the atonement the Lord Jesus had made and raised Him from the dead and highly exalted Him. Where the head is, there the body must also be. The sinner is joined forever to his Savior, with whom God is well pleased. By this means the woman received peace with God through Jesus Christ.

A Woman in Samuel Miller's Congregation

Dr. Samuel Miller was the preacher in Free St. Matthew's Church in Glasgow, and one week Brownlow North was taking meetings in his church. He called in at Samuel Miller's study looking very weary and asking if they could go for a walk. What was wrong? He had spent much of the day talking to people who were very concerned about their relationship with God, but one woman in particular had occupied an hour and a half of the evangelist's time. She was in considerable distress, telling North that the Lord had given her up. Brownlow spoke to her, but nothing could dent her conviction that the Lord would have nothing to do with her and would not hear her prayers.

Then Brownlow North asked her, "Are you a believer? Have you placed your trust in God?" She replied affirmatively. "And the Lord has given you up?" "Yes." "Then," said the evangelist, "either you or he must be a liar. Are you telling me a lie just now when you say you have placed your trust in Christ?" "No, certainly not." "Then the Lord must be a liar, and in that case if I were you, I would give him up!" "Oh, but I can't give him up, sir." "Why not? If he is a liar." "I can't give him up." "Ah," said Brownlow North, "That is because the Lord has not given you up." And the realization of the truth of that word sank in and established in her a renewed trust in the Lord. North had excellent spiritual perception and shrewdness so that he understood the muddles people were making of their own lives, and he could adapt his counsels to their condition.

A Man from Edinburgh

One Sunday a man made his way to a meeting after the service in St. Luke's, where he confronted Brownlow North. "Sir, I've listened to your sermon. I've often heard you preach, but I neither care for you nor your sermons. You must answer one question for me, why did God permit sin in the world?" "I will tell you," replied the evangelist immediately. "God permitted sin because he chose to do so." The man was taken aback at the immediate response. It seemed to throw little light on his question. "Because he chose to do so," Brownlow repeated, and then he added,

> And if you continue to question and cavil at God's dealings, and vainly puffed up by your carnal mind strive to be wise above what is written, I will tell you something more that God will choose to do. He will some day choose to put you into hell. It is vain, sir, for man to strive with his Maker. You cannot resist him, and neither your opinion of his dealings nor your blasphemous expression of them will in the least lessen the pain of your everlasting damnation which will most certainly be your portion if you go on in your present spirit. There were such questioners as you in Paul's time and what the apostle said to them I say to you, "Nay, but, O man, who art thou that repliest against God?"

The young man, much subdued, said to him, "Is there such a text, sir, as that in the Bible?" "Yes, there is," replied the evangelist. "It is in the ninth chapter of Romans. I recommend you to go home and read it and learn from God's own word that God claims for himself the right to do whatever he chooses, and does not permit the thing formed to say to him that formed it, Why hast thou made me thus? But you remember also this, that besides permitting sin there is another thing that God has chosen to do, *God chose to send Jesus.*" In a few words he then pointed out to the young man the way of salvation revealed so clearly in God's Word, a way that magnifies the wonderful grace and mercy of God to rebel, disdainful, unworthy sinners, and he urged the young man to receive this salvation and this Redeemer into his life as Lord and Savior.

Five days later in the St. Luke's manse, it was announced that there was a young man who wished to talk to Brownlow North. He readily agreed and met the man. "Do you remember me?" he asked the evangelist, but he could not. "Don't you remember the man who on Sunday night asked you to tell him why God permitted sin?" "Ah, yes, perfectly," Brownlow replied. "I am he," said the man, "and you said to me that God permitted sin because he chose to do so, and you told me to go home and read the ninth chapter of Romans, and you also told me that God chose to send Jesus to die for such sinners as I was. Well, I went home, and I did, sir, exactly what you told me." He had gone home and read Romans 9 and then pleaded for forgiveness in Jesus's name, and for the gift of the Holy Spirit to be his teacher. Soon afterward he was enabled to believe that he had been heard and pardoned. "Now I am happy, sir, oh I am so happy, and though the devil comes sometimes to tempt me with my old thoughts, and to ask me what *reason* I have to think that God has forgiven me, I always manage to get him away by telling him that I do not want to judge things any longer by my own reason but by God's word. The only reason why I know I am forgiven, I tell him, is that for God's sake, God chooses to pardon me."

Brownlow North recounted the story to Dr. Moody-Stuart and his family, explaining that he did not remember the man after just five days because the man's countenance had changed so remarkably in that time, the haughtiness and unbelief being replaced by a radiance of joy and peace in believing. The story spread through Edinburgh and reached Principal Cunningham, who listened attentively with much appreciation. "That shows me that Brownlow North knows what he's about," he said. The encounter even became one of the evangelist's powerful tracts, "God Chose to Send Jesus."

A Woman Living Near Scotscraig

A woman came to talk to Brownlow North, but she seemed to lack earnestness as she spoke to him. He told her that she should think of all that the world had to offer her. "Now, are you prepared to give up all of that and take Christ?" She thought for a moment and then shook her head. "I cannot say that. But you did say something in last night's meeting that has troubled me and made me anxious." Brownlow let that hang in the air for a moment and then said, "It would be a mockery for you to go to the Lord Jesus and say to him that you want him to come down and dwell in your heart if there is anything else that you are preferring to him. I could not help you. I could not pray with you in those circum-stances." The woman was offended and got up sadly to leave him. As she was walking to the door, he called after her, "Think what those idols that you are preferring to Christ can do for you at your dying hour, and remember that I will be delighted to see you again when you have decided to take Jesus Christ as your Lord."

So this young and beautiful woman left him. He did not expect to see her again, but four days later she called on him, this time lacking the whole buoyancy and confidence of her earlier visit. She was so pale and downcast that he scarcely recognized her. "Sir, I have had a terrible time, and awful struggle since I was last with you. I have just one question for you today. I've come to ask you whether you think Christ will take me." That was an easy counseling session for Brownlow North as he took the young woman to the Lord and His promises. He would say, "The only plea the Psalmist ever seems to make for himself is that he is poor and needy. He never pleads his repentance, or his sorrow, or anything he has. Simply, 'I have nothing.'" In her first visit the question had been whether she would take Christ, and she had been unwilling to do so if it meant His priority over all the things she loved and valued most. Now the question was whether the Lord of glory, the King of Kings, was prepared to take her as His eternal friend and heir. When she was shown the warrant of faith, the promises of rest for those who would come to Him, and the promise of eternal life for those who believed in Him, her difficulty was removed.

A week later he met her walking in the street to his house. "I was on my way to see you to tell you of the joy and peace I have found in believing in the Lord Jesus," she said. "I have known such a time of delight in talking with him and thinking of all he has done for me—so much lasting pleasure than all I'd got from the world." Months later North received news that she had experienced a burst blood vessel and had died within ten minutes. He exclaimed, "Wasn't it well for her that she had chosen the Lord Christ and not the pleasures of the world as her portion?"

A Sheep Farmer in the Australian Outback

A Scottish teenager left school and plunged into an anti-Christian lifestyle of excess and crime. Arrested, tried, and found guilty, he was sentenced to be shipped off to Australia at the age of twenty-one. For the next fifteen years, he never entered a place of worship, except on one occasion when a church served as a polling place. The only times he would pray were on the rare occasions when he was lost or in danger or sick from his excessive drinking. He lived in a remote shepherd's hut, far from any other people, and would go for months without meeting another human being. The loneliness got to him, and he asked God to help him. Soon he began sharing a larger hut with another shepherd.

Life was more pleasant, but he still had not found peace and happiness. He felt convicted that he had neglected his promise to serve God if He would provide him better circumstances. One time his companion had taken some of the herd to another pasture, and he was in the hut alone. He fell on his knees and prayed to God for forgiveness for wasting his life and failing to serve Him. There was no Bible in the place, but there was a copy of Brownlow North's *Earnest Words*. His companion had a Christian sister in Scotland who was praying for him, and she had sent him the little book. He eagerly picked it up and slowly read the chapters. In reading these tracts he found the way of salvation and peace through believing in the Lord Jesus.

His companion returned later that day, and he told him that he had become a Christian and about the help he had received in reading the book the man's sister had sent to him. The man himself began to read it and was also converted. That book was never out of the hands of either of them in the months ahead until they were able to purchase a Bible. Each day they decided which one would have *Earnest Words*. They parted a few months later, and he began working and living with a group of men who like himself had been shipped off to Australia as punishment for their crimes. They were twenty to thirty in number, the most profligate of men, but the Lord strengthened him, and they all saw him kneeling and praying in the dormitory each night. He decided to write to Brownlow North, care of the publisher, and so North came to hear of this new servant of God in the Australian outback. How true were the evangelist's words regarding the history of this man's fall: "The devil wants us to commit no greater sin than to forget God."

The Wife of a Member of Parliament

A woman converted through the ministry of Brownlow North explained to her sister, the wife of a member of Parliament, the change that God had wrought in her life. She too became an earnest Christian and occasionally invited her husband's work colleagues to dinner at their home. She was planning the next gathering when she talked to her husband about a woman related to her who was bitterly opposed to the ministry of Brownlow North. In her relative's eyes the man was a killjoy, creating a guilt complex about innocent pleasures. He was so negative, stealing joy from Christians. There was no way she could imagine her relative coming to a dinner party where Brownlow North was one of the guests. She was sitting in the living room with a list of guests in front of her and a pile of invitation cards. She looked at her husband and said, "We need not ask my cousin; she won't come." Her husband raised his eyebrows and shrugged, "Ask her. If she does not come then that is her affair. You do your duty." So she sent her cousin an invitation, praying over it much, and the invitation was accepted. At the dinner Brownlow North spoke of his faith and commended to them all his Savior, and this woman's cousin was affected and awakened to a sense of sin and danger. She requested a personal conversation with him in the following weeks, and he helped her to come to personal trust in the Savior. She was soon after taken seriously ill, but through that time she found peace and comfort through continuing to rest in Christ.

Chapter 15

His Directness in Evangelism

Brownlow North distinguished between those whose hopes were in the Lord Jesus and those who were lost. Hear him speak on Christ becoming a curse for us:

> Should God say to you tonight, I will forgive all your sins except the least sin you ever did, what would you do with that one sin? Soon the world shall have passed away. Then there will be but two places for you. Could you take that sin into heaven with you? The curse of God would be upon you. For that one sin you must depart from God. Is the curse on you, or has it been laid on Christ for you? He was made a curse on that moment when he cried, "My God! My God! Why hast thou forsaken me?" His soul was then made an offering for sin. He was alive to feel the curse. Nothing ever wrung from him such a cry but God forsaking him. He poured out his soul unto death. He was forsaken that we might be visited in mercy.

Brownlow North preached the substitutionary atonement of Christ; that is, He died in place of those whose hopes and trust are all in Him. He died for our sins. He became a curse for us. But His death for us is just one part of the message. He also lived for us. He spent thirty-three years magnifying the law and fulfilling all righteousness for us. Now He is the end of our law keeping and is our way of obtaining divine righteousness. So Brownlow North declared to sinners not only Christ's sacrifice on the cross but also the righteousness of His life. Hear how he directly addresses them:

Accept his blood and righteousness, and be made the righteousness of God in him. Strip off all the filthy rags, all your own feelings, prayers and good deals. Come naked and foul, wash in the pool of the Saviour's blood, and then, clean yet unprofitable, put on the robe of righteousness, be covered over with the Saviour's life, that the blessing may come on you. It is not Jesus' blood alone but his good works also that are reckoned ours as our bad works were reckoned his. He worked for his people, and his life is imputed to us, as ours was to him.

You may have a righteousness that is as perfect as God's. Where did the thief get it? Where did Paul get it? Be covered with the thoughts, the words, the actions of Jesus, as he was covered with your thoughts and words, and actions in God's first sight when he was made a curse for you. The Christian is as hell-deserving the day he dies as the day he first believes. Each week is mixed with sin. Were he to be judged at the last by his best work then he would be condemned.

Then the sinner must close with Christ as our Saviour and our all. Christ gave himself for all who give themselves to him. Give your past to Jesus. You take Jesus past and then you can say Jesus has got me. All my past life I give to him. Give your present self to Christ, quite unreservedly. Take Christ present as Saviour and Lord, as wisdom, righteousness, sanctification, and redemption to you. Then remember, I am not my own. Sin is not my own, Christ has taken it. Give your future to Christ and take the future of Christ as the portion of your soul. You shall see him as he is. You shall be satisfied when you awake with his likeness. Have you loved his appearing? Now we are no more slaves but soldiers. We must fight and pray, but when he comes the fight will be over and we shall hear the words "Well done, good and faithful servant, enter thou into the joy of thy Lord." Let me ask you whether this is true. That Christ the Lord offer himself, past, present and future to you? Is this true that Christ is willing and able to save you in particular and that he offers to save you now. Alas, is it also true that you say you won't take him?

Again he spoke directly when taking domestic and family prayers. James Balfour recounts one particular incident:

I remember once in a house where several had been asked to meet him he began by opening the Bible and saying, "none of you know where I am going to read tonight, do you? No you don't. And you never will till I tell you. I am going to read in 1 Corinthians, but again you don't know what chapter.... I am going to read the first chapter of the epistle. You know now because I have told you. You did not find it out for yourselves. There was not one of you clever enough to do this. The only reason you know is because I chose to tell you. Now this is the principle upon which the apostle's argument in this chapter proceeds. He tells us straight that 'The world by wisdom knew not God.' None of the princes of this world knew that Jesus was the Lord of glory or they would not have crucified him. God was determined that no man should find him out by his own wits. God has revealed them to us by his Spirit; 'for the Spirit searches all things, yes, the deep things of God.'" He was intimate and direct as he spoke.

Brownlow North was just as direct in his personal counseling as he was in the pulpit. This is a typical dialogue:

"Has God forgiven you?"

"I dare not say he has."

"Have you asked him?"

"Yes."

"Do you wish to be God's child, and to give up sin?"

"Oh yes, sir, God knows that I wish to be Christ's only."

"And you are not?"

"No sir."

"But you are blessed."

"Oh no, sir."

"Then the Bible is not true."

"Oh yes, it is."

"But what does the Bible say of the state of those who hunger and thirst after righteousness?"

"Sir, it says that they are blessed."

"Then aren't you blessed?"

"Sir, I am afraid to say that I am."

"But if God says you are, who is it who says you're not? Isn't it the devil?"

"Oh yes, sir. He must be the liar. I do hunger and thirst after righteousness."

"Then you are blessed for God has promised that you shall be filled."

Such direct counseling was the means of giving great peace to the person being counseled. It is always so. It had been Puritan counseling, and the inheritance of the Reformation leaders.

To be holy is to be a partaker of the divine nature, devoted to God and appropriated to Him, His will, and His use. It is to have hearts and lives that are not common and unclean. To be godly is to live to God, as those from their hearts believe that He is God indeed and that He is "the rewarder of them that diligently seek him," that He is our God all-sufficient, our "shield, and...exceeding great reward," and that "of him, and through him, and to him, are all things," that all may give glory to Him for ever and for ever. God should be first, and last, and all in the mind, mouth, and life of a believer. God must be the principal matter in your religion. The understanding and will must be exercised on Him

Chapter 16

Some Scenes from His Last Years of Itinerant Evangelism

Brownlow North was now the most respected evangelist in the United Kingdom. He not only related an extraordinary story of conversion but also had an awakening ministry everywhere he went, and now he was at the height of his influence. In 1868 the fifty-eight-year-old Brownlow North went to Wales via a brief visit to Birmingham, where he had many invitations to return.

In Swansea

Just nine years after the 1859 revival, North preached in Swansea's vast music hall. There was a longing that God would move again, and the evangelist gave his impressions to a friend in the days following of that extraordinary meeting:

> I am sure you will rejoice with me when you hear that last night I had a meeting which to my own feelings was the most encouraging one I have had for years. It was in the Music Hall, an enormous place with double galleries, holding thousands. I went under the idea that there would not be a hundred people there, but it was crammed, hundreds

standing on the floor of the lower hall. Many of the upper classes were there, and a more solemnized congregation I have seldom seen. Indeed, I hope Swansea is at least moved. I am very sanguine that much real good was done. The people seemed taken aback as if it were all new to them. I believe I spoke with power. I came home softened, and cried like a child. Today the impression remains on me, and I feel at peace with God. Oh, may the peace never be again broken. May he lead, and I follow.

How would you describe such preaching? Perhaps that rivers of living water flowed out of the evangelist's inmost being? Those meetings went on for a week, and again he wrote,

I have to tell you of such a meeting! The last day has been the great day of the feast. Yesterday it was blowing a gale of wind and raining hard at the time of the meeting, and I did not think it possible I could have any people to speak to. Yet, though the storm continued, I found the place crammed, and it certainly is an enormous place. It being the last night I had determined to have a second address for inquirers. I began, and so far as sympathy goes, I felt that as I warmed, the people warmed, and I spoke to an audience that was almost breathless through interest for the whole time, for two hours and ten minutes. So far as I can judge I have not spoken so for years, but the issue is with the Lord.

In Birmingham

In the spring of 1870 the evangelist returned to Birmingham, where John Angell James had been the preacher in

Carrs Lane Congregational Church for fifty-five years. It was his one ministry, but he was joined by a co-pastor, R. W. Dale, in 1853, who became sole pastor and James's successor in 1859. Dale's message was so different from John Angell James's. It was a message of "civic gospel," with its concern for the living conditions of the thousands who had moved into Birmingham to work in the various industries. People were being told that new conditions in the Midlands required this new message.

However, there were still thousands in Birmingham who remembered with longing the gospel ministry of Angell James. So in the spring of 1870 Brownlow North began his preaching, and evangelical Christians were given cause to rejoice again at the preaching of the gospel. The evangelist wrote to his friend,

> Last night was wonderful. Loads of young men were unable to get in, and they were just the kind I wanted. Hundreds of them were, I should judge, thoroughly "fast" young men, but they behaved very well; first, they were quiet, and then attentive, then solemnized. The only disturbance was from one or two fainting from the heat. I preached in my fur coat! At the end a paper was handed up to me, begging for another address which I announced for Friday the 25th amidst loud cheers—which I stopped. I don't, however, expect to get another such meeting. We shall see. I am rather headachy, as you can imagine after last night. I forgot to say that I preached for an hour and a half fully. Too long for speakers…or hearers!

Then, of the closing meeting of his ministry in Birmingham, he wrote,

I must send you a line on my last day in Birmingham, my visit, of which I cannot but think that it has been of much moment to many. Two men have just left me who found me in consequence of last night's meeting. It was a very remarkable one. The enormous place was full; mostly men—many of them quite the rougher sort, who all sat, about 3,000 of them, deeply attentive for over an hour's sermon. I do think that good has been done here. A man from North Wales wants to translate *The Rich Man and Lazarus* into Welsh.

In London

In 1870 North began to seek a house in London, and the following year he moved from Elgin to a beautiful place called The Knoll. At this time the London meetings were held in St. James's Hall in London. After the service, Sir Thomas Beauchamp got General Russell to introduce North. He wanted to tell the evangelist that an old shooting friend of North's who owned much land in Scotland had been impressed by one of his books and would like to see him. The evangelist wrote to the Earl of Kintore, telling him of the meeting: "I agreed to go and dine with him some day. It was at that moment that a young man came into the waiting room, a clerk in H. and I's to tell me that I had been the means of saving his soul when I was last in London. When he left the room Fishbourne told me that he had been the means of bringing hundreds of others to the Lord since his conversion. All this is very pleasing."

In the next day or two, he met his old companion at dinner. The ladies left after the meal, and Brownlow began a very personal conversation about eternal things with him and the men who had remained. Finally, he asked them all if they would kneel down, and Brownlow led them in prayer. His friend was intending in the next days to go on a long cruise on his yacht, but he delayed his departure to hear the evangelist preaching.

It was at this time that Brownlow heard that his great friend and supporter, Sir James Simpson, had died, and he wrote to one of the family saying, "I am sorry for you, sorry for your mother, sorry for his family, sorry for myself, sorry for Edinburgh, sorry for the country, but not sorry for him."

In Plymouth

Brownlow's trip to Plymouth was his first visit so far south in England. The church he preached in on a Sunday night was packed to suffocation. He prayed for God's blessing on the meeting, and then the vicar unexpectedly climbed the pulpit steps and told the congregation that several hundred people were standing locked outside. North got up and addressed the congregation, asking them to squeeze together as near as they could to the person next to them. Then the doors were unlocked and another hundred were allowed in.

A dignitary in the Church of England was preaching in a nearby church that evening. Some of those present had heard the man peddling quite heretical ideas in the morning service, so that evening Brownlow North explained the gospel and exposed the man's errors. When the evening ended he was given a letter from a young woman describing God's dealings with her:

My parents are ungodly, living utterly careless of their souls; they do not even pray to God, or say prayers at any time. I never heard them utter a word of prayer in my life. I don't think they ever think of their souls. I have tried to get them to come and hear you, but have not succeeded. Oh, pray for them! I have *not one* Christian relative. I have one or two Christian friends, but I have never been able to have Christian intercourse with them. I have often tried but of no avail, and I never felt that I could pour out my heart to an earthly friend before I heard you.

Then I thought I could tell you everything, God grant that I may (as you are leaving) have someone with whom I can have Christian intercourse! I do not know how to express myself. My soul is overwhelmed with love to Christ. I never felt nor thought in my whole life as I do now, and have done so ever since I heard you preach of Christ. Yes, I know God, our heavenly Father, did specially send you to me. You have by your preaching, thrown fresh life across my mind, you have caused my eyes to open, and my ears to hear, and my heart to understand the boundless love of God towards us, his tenderness and his compassion. You have, by the Spirit of the Lord, caused me to understand more of the love of Christ Jesus our Lord. You have caused me to put my whole trust in Jesus, and to cast myself utterly and completely on him. I shall never, never forget you.

God used Brownlow North to awaken sinners, that is indeed true, but North also, as a debtor to the loving kindness of God, communicated the sweetness and infinite fullness of the grace of God. This was particularly so in the latter mellowing years of his ministry.

In Edinburgh

When a Lord's Day in Edinburgh came to an end, one of his hearers went home, sat down, and wrote to him thus:

Dear Sir,

Will you pardon the liberty a stranger takes in writing to you? I do humbly and earnestly ask an interest in your prayers. Will you pray to God that he may convert me to himself? I have several times had the privilege of hearing you preach in Edinburgh. The first time was a few years ago. Then I was happy with my beloved mother and my brothers and sisters. Now my mother and all my sisters lie in the silent tomb beside my father. My brothers are all scattered, and I am left alone, almost without a friend in the world. After our home was broken up I went out as a governess, but at present I am again in search of a situation. Oh, dear Mr. North, will you pray for me, that though I am deprived of all my earthly family, I may belong to the family of God, and not myself only, but also my three dear brothers? Do pray for us. Again I ask your forgiveness for addressing you. And that every blessing both temporal and spiritual may be vouchsafed to you and yours is the earnest desire of a young woman who loves and respects you.

This is a man whom Christian women were drawn to in absolute trust, opening their lives to him and desiring his counsels and prayers. He never once betrayed their affection by taking advantage of it in any untoward way.

His love was from a pure and holy heart where Jesus Christ reigned, filled with a fervent Christian affection.

On one occasion he encountered a young woman who once had been drawn to the Christian life but had turned back. She now wanted to turn away from the arid life of unbelief and went to see the evangelist. In speaking with her, he came to believe that she was looking too much into her own heart to seek assurance of salvation. She thought she needed to reach a certain standard of living and believing before she could trust in Christ, and so she fell increasingly into despair. After one of North's meetings in Edinburgh, she came to talk to him. The conversation between them was very brief:

He said to her, "Are you saved?"

She said, "No."

He said, "Why not?"

She said, "Because I do not feel that I love Jesus."

He said, "That does not matter. What's most important is that He loves you."

She said nothing more. He said nothing more. No more needed to be said. What she needed was to trust in the dying and living love of the Lord Christ for her, which she then saw and which she then once definitively, and then continually embraced for the rest of her days; it was a useful and happy life.

In Bournemouth

Brownlow North was a friend of Adolph Saphir, the Jewish Presbyterian author and missionary. Saphir had been born in Budapest, the son of a leading member of the Jewish community. In 1843, his whole family—father, mother, sister and brothers—were converted to Christianity through "Rabbi" John Duncan's witness, and they were all baptized. Duncan was a great supporter of Brownlow North, but he was there in eastern Europe as part of the Jewish mission of the Church of Scotland, which had been supported by M'Cheyne and the Bonar brothers, among many others. Saphir persuaded Brownlow North to hold a series of meetings in Bournemouth in the spring of 1873. North wrote to a friend describing his time there:

> Such a whirl at Bournemouth! Yet I believe it was a very blessed time. The dear old Baron with whom I was staying certainly seemed to get good. The last morning at prayers he wept like a child. He said afterwards, "Oh! You naughty man! You have made me cry! I had left that to my wife!" Then, as a large vase of beautiful flowers was brought into the room, he said, "Ah, they are very beautiful…but it is North that has strewn my path with flowers." To God be all the glory! The Baron's was only one case among many. I came here on Saturday to preach for Saphir last Sunday. The church was very full, and the people attentive. I will preach for him again, God willing, next Sunday. Then on the following Sunday I am at Cambridge.

Six weeks after his time in Bournemouth, North received a letter from a young woman who had heard him there:

> Indeed I am wonderfully happy and blessed in my

new and precious possession. I am trying to make everybody I meet be the same. Oh the joy you will have in heaven when many, many point to you as the means of their conversion. How I pray that I may never be cast away. I am learning a great deal of my precious Bible now. Six weeks ago was to me the beginning of days when you preached in Mr. Saphir's in the evening. It was then I determined, God helping me, to give up my whole heart to Jesus Christ.

In his final years North continued preaching the sermons he had preached with much effect at the beginning of his ministry, though in his midweek and house meeting, he was constantly preparing new studies of the Word of God. One of his last acts was to present to Christians a new hall in a part of Elgin where he had his home for many years. He regretted that he had not been a more faithful evangelist to his own neighbors, and so this hall was erected and prepared for gospel ministry and would be so used when he went to live in London.

Chapter 17

His Ultimate Year of Preaching in Glasglow

However much Brownlow North loved his house in London, his love for the people of Scotland was a greater draw on his gifts. As he grew increasingly weaker, he dedicated his remaining energy to preaching the gospel of Jesus Christ. Although opportunities were presented to him in England, his love of the people of Scotland opened hundreds of pulpits to him and full congregations of eager hearers. He was most at home where he had begun his ministry, so at the end of 1874 and the beginning of 1875, he evangelized Glasgow. He was suffering with constant colds and a feeling of exhaustion, but once he stood at the pulpit and faced a congregation of expectant hearers, his weakness vanished. How careful he was to nurture himself through the day before his evening labors.

However, now he had a famous colaborer, D. L. Moody, who was also invited to Glasgow with his companion, the hearty tenor Ira D. Sankey. The city was divided between them, with Brownlow preaching in Govan, Partick, and Hillhead. The meetings in the latter district were held in Kelvinside Free Church, and on the first Sunday, in a

show of genuine affection and unity that the two men had
for one another, Moody preached in the morning a chal-
lenging call to everyone to witness for their Lord on the
text "to every man his work" (Mark 13:34). In the evening
North spoke fervently and solemnly on the rich man and
Lazarus. In the following weeks he preached new sermons
from the Psalms on alternate weeknight meetings. At the
close of the Lord's Day, between four hundred and five
hundred people attended prayer meetings. In the weeks
ahead, Brownlow North preached with great effect to
packed congregations at Barony Free Church. He glowed
with vigor as he engaged in particular with hard-headed
men who had long refused to receive Christ the Lord, and
several of them bowed before him.

How did Brownlow North respond to D. L. Moody?
This was the first time he had met the American whose
fame was all over the United Kingdom. He was "the new
kid on the block," and his novelty was enhanced by having
the tenor Ira D. Sankey sing solos in his services, accompanied by an organ or piano. All this was quite attractive
to many people. On top of this, Moody's meetings were
very well organized. But the British evangelist did not
have an envious bone in his body. He believed and hoped
all things. He rejoiced to hear the gospel preached, and
he met new Christians who had been converted through
Moody's ministry. His trusted old friends spoke well of the
meetings where they had observed the American's preaching. Moody heard Brownlow North preach just once in
Glasgow, saying he would never forget the sermon, and

they also spoke together and showed interested in each other's lives.

North wrote to numbers of his friends expressing his delight in Moody's arrival. In one letter to a particularly close friend, the Earl of Kintore, he reveals his precarious health and deep appreciation of Moody's preaching:

My Dearest Kintore,

I am getting older and uglier and deafer every year, not attractions with which to make new friends. So I am more jealous of the old one, and I should be sorry to many of them if I could help it, and none more so than yourself, dear Kintore, for we have travelled together as friends over many a long year or good report and evil report. My ending, I suspect, is not very far off, for I am full of gout and rheumatism, added to which Sir William Gull, whom I consulted, says I have a weak heart and enlarged liver....

The success of Moody and Sankey is a miracle, perfectly superhuman! Every service crammed, and after every service the inquiry room also. Of course the devil rages, as he always does when God works, and he is working, I most firmly believe, *mightily....* The whole household has gone tonight to hear Moody and Sankey.... I am so glad that one we both know got such a blessing from them. May the Lord increase it more and more.

Always and ever yours, most affectionately,
Brownlow North

At the end of one of Brownlow North's services in Glasgow, a man who was training to be an engineer came to speak to him, telling him that some months earlier he had been converted when hearing him preach in another church in the city. He had been for a walk while visiting a friend on a Sunday afternoon, and they passed by a church where it was announced that North would be preaching that night. They decided to enter and hear him. Brownlow's text was, "But we preach Christ crucified, unto the Jews a stumblingblock, and unto the Greeks foolishness; but unto them which are called, both Jews and Greeks, Christ the power of God, and the wisdom of God" (1 Cor. 1:23, 24).

This man had left the service unchanged except for the mustard seed of a thought that began to grow. If what those verses said was true, then so far he had been a fool by thinking that belief in Jesus Christ was foolishness. He mulled over that information as he walked home with his friend, but the ideas that had started as a provocative thought quickly gained in power and agitated him as they crossed the river Clyde. He soon felt that all the demons from the pit were pressing in on him, so much so that he stopped in the middle of the bridge and decided that this matter had to be settled there and then, in one way or the other, before he had crossed over the Clyde. He knew he would face the jeers of his former friends if he told them that he had been converted, but he was faced with this life-changing decision of whether he would take Christ and henceforth follow Him as his God. He breathed deeply and then accepted Christ, and in a moment he knew a joy that words could not express. The inner storms abated and he had rest; indeed, he felt so light that he thought his feet were not touching the pavement. And now, he told North, Jesus Christ is still to him the wisdom and the power of God.

Brownlow North made a few inquiries as to where the student came from, and with his encyclopedic knowledge of Scotland, he realized who he was. "I know you. I knew your father." His father had been a minister in Morayshire, and soon after North had begun preaching, he was asked to speak in this man's church, but the minister died suddenly before he had opportunity to do so. Brownlow came and preached at his funeral, where this student, then a little boy, had been present. Sixteen years had elapsed, and now the Good Shepherd had found the boy and brought him to hear the man who had preached at his dad's funeral service. Now He was assuring him there on the Clyde bridge that he was one of His sheep. The little group listening to this moving history finally got up to leave the church, and a friend offered to help Brownlow put on his coat. He took it from him and handed it over to the engineering student, saying, "Let my child help me on with it."

Around this time Brownlow North broke one of his own rules. He never remained in the church to talk to anxious inquirers after the meeting. He was in a sweat, exhausted, and liable to be chilled. Throughout his life he nursed himself very carefully, and his friends would tease him about his scrupulousness. Each night at the end of the meeting, he would put on his coat and soon leave for home, but one evening in Glasgow he was specially requested to stay and talk to some people. There in an unheated room he caught a chill and was confined to bed with other complications. He was to preach the next day, and the church was full. He insisted on traveling there in a cab, covered in blankets, but an eruption of boils meant he could not sit down. He kneeled on the floor of the cab for the journey. He could not sit in the church, and after his preaching he traveled back home in the cab, again kneeling on the floor. God blessed the word that night, and though his friends cautioned him about continuing, he pursued that same plan of kneeling on the floor of the cab and standing through the service on three occasions each week for the next month. He was then sixty-three years of age. A doctor who examined him in a few months' time, shortly before he died, told him that his heart was so weakened that he might at any point have dropped dead in the pulpit. All of Scotland, hearing of his illness, especially the thousands who knew him to be their spiritual father, prayed for him. "Help, LORD; for the godly man ceaseth; for the faithful fail from among the children of men" (Ps. 12:1).

Like most men who have dietary requirements and uncertain health, Brownlow North had his own little ways and preferences. He was often away from home, staying in different manses and attended to by different women. If someone has discomforts that last for only a day or two, they can be endured without a word, but if one stays somewhere for a month, there is a need to be frank concerning details. But Brownlow North was sensitive about causing trouble, and he would introduce himself to his host by saying, "I am afraid that you have in your home today a very troublesome guest." His closest friends would urge him not to say things like that, because he was building up an untrue picture of himself. "There are enough people hostile to your message who would seize those words of yours and spread the rumour that you are an awkward customer." In fact, he was a genial and delightful guest with a kind and grateful manner, thoroughly concerned for those whose duty it was to look after him. Most of his hosts regarded it an enormous privilege to have Brownlow North to stay with them for a time.

Chapter 18

Last Days and Death

Brownlow North packed an incredible amount of work into the twenty years following his conversion, more than most gospel servants of God achieve in fifty. He was a good soldier of Jesus Christ, taking the initiative in assaulting the fashionable confidences of the proponents of liberalism. He did not stand on the defensive but rather took the fight to those who were beginning to preach another gospel.

His health was giving way as he approached the end of his earthly course, and he would express some nervousness about the act of dying, but then would add, "We are in the world, and must go out of it." Once, when staying at someone's home, he was without warning asked to conduct family worship. He had not thought of it and expressed his perplexity to a friend. That man told him, "Yes, but the Lord is with us," to which North promptly answered, "Ah, but we are not always with him." He was conscious of a felt need of the helpful presence of God in his life. He increasingly referred to himself in his prayers at this time as "this poor sinner," and he had become more conscious of the marvelous grace that had called him from darkness into light and had made him a chosen vessel for God's service. His own call by the mercy of Christ was always a vivid reality to him, and tears were never far away.

As the end drew near, he enjoyed a week at Humbie and was in particularly good spirits, taking interest in all the agricultural activities of the place. He preached in Kelso parish church to a full congregation, speaking earnestly on one of his favorite passages. He was to hold meetings at Alexandria in Dunbartonshire, and then a Mr. Campbell of Tullichewan Castle on the banks of Loch Lomond invited him to be his guest there. He was a complete stranger to the castle and the Campbell family. In fact, they had not been the most sympathetic regarding his doctrinal convictions and emphases, but they grew to respect him while he spent his last days under their roof. Mrs. Campbell said, "He came to us as a stranger. Some of us were prejudiced against him, but he won all our hearts and also won our belief that he was a sincere and earnest Christian."

Brownlow preached on Sunday, the following Wednesday, and Friday to almost seven hundred people, with his final address being on Psalm 86, which ends, "But thou, O Lord, art a God full of compassion, and gracious, long suffering, and plenteous in mercy and truth. O turn unto me, and have mercy upon me; give thy strength unto thy servant, and save the son of thine handmaid. Shew me a token for good; that they which hate me may see it, and be ashamed: because thou, LORD, hast holpen me, and comforted me."

In the next days he took family devotions and preached three more times in the local church, but it was now an exhausting business. He would return to the castle, go to his room, and not emerge until 5 p.m. the next day. On Saturday he was taken ill. The guest in the next bedroom heard the thump of his fall, and finding him on the floor, he hurriedly got him into bed. The evangelist was kept as quiet as possible, and his wife was sent for. His final illness lasted for ten days, and she never left until the end. Friends came to see him, but there were days when he was in a deep sleep, although sometimes he would rally and could identify them and say their names.

During that period he said, "I used to have a great terror of death, but that is quite gone from me. I have no fear of it now. I am resting in Christ." He turned to another standing at his bedside and said, "You are a young man and in good health and with the prospect of promotion in the army. I am dying, but if the Bible is true, and I know it is, I would not change places with you for the whole world."

James Balfour sat with him, and Brownlow held his hand, able to speak only in whispers and with considerable effort. He said to James, "Jesus came to me and he said, 'I will never leave thee nor forsake thee.' And up to this time he never has…but I have been a beast." James said to him, "I have often thought that the verse on which I would like to die is, 'The blood of Jesus Christ His Son cleanseth us from all sin.'" "That," the old evangelist replied, "is the verse on which I am dying. One wants no more." "This dying," said James, "is what you and I have often spoken of." "Often," Brownlow replied. "Have you peace?" he asked him. "Perfect peace," he said with much meaning.

James prayed, and Brownlow wiped his eyes. The next day he breathed his last breath.

At his funeral, 1 Corinthians 15 was read and a paraphrase of it was sung:

> How bright those glorious spirits shine!
>   Whence all their white array?
> How came they to the blissful seats of
>   everlasting day?
> Lo these are they from sufferings great who came
>   to realms of light,
> And in the blood of Christ have washed those robes,
>   which shine so bright.

Old friends prayed and read Scripture at the service. His remains were laid in the tomb beside his daughter-in-law, and his tombstone reads as follows:

BROWNLOW NORTH
ONLY SON OF THE
REV. CHARLES AUGUSTUS NORTH
Prebendary of Winchester

BORN JANUARY 6TH 1810:
DIED NOVEMBER 9TH, 1873

At the age of forty-four he was turned from an ungodly life to serve the Lord; thereafter he preached the gospel with singular power, and was greatly honoured in winning souls to Jesus.

IN TESTIMONY OF THE LOVE AND
RESPECT OF MANY FRIENDS

Kenneth Moody-Stuart mentioned that some critics of the evangelist used the fact of the two contrasting halves of his life to question the wisdom of the divine procedures that permitted such a man to live an utterly selfish life for forty years and then chose to convert him for a further twenty years of evangelistic activity. They might as well challenge the divine grace that saved a dying criminal hanging on the cross alongside the Savior. Why didn't God convert the man before he became a vile criminal? All we can say is, "Even so, Father: for so it seemed good in thy sight."

God more than conquered this defiant, selfish aristocrat. He did not save him so that for the rest of his life he might live as a quiet gardener and churchgoer. He conquered North to become a mighty evangelist, a glorious trophy of grace, that no one in Scotland might despair.

Thus the Lord has done throughout church history. The Reformer Theodore Beza one day heard an opponent scornfully throwing his sins in his face. Beza shouted out, "This man envies me Christ's grace!" The church father Augustine of Hippo replied to a man who had pointed out his previous lifestyle of sin, "The more desperate was my disease the greater honor resounded to the physician who cured me." Let us not despair of those who yet live while they have long defied God and His gospel. The early church must have considered Saul of Tarsus the very last person in the world to become an evangelist of Jesus Christ and a church planter. So it must have seemed to those churchgoers on their way to morning worship when middle-aged Brownlow North and his companions rode past with their rifles, off for a day's shooting, yet it would not be long before they would be hearing him humbly teach them the gospel of Jesus Christ. "See what God has wrought," they cried. We cry with them.

A Note on the Sources

This book would not be possible without the definitive and delightful biography of Kenneth Moody-Stuart, who knew and loved Brownlow North and whose father was a pastor and earnest supporter of the great evangelist. I make no claims to originality. I have based my story on his work, the first edition of which appeared in 1878. I have used Moody-Stuart's first edition extensively, but I have omitted those references for the sake of the readers' enjoyment and to keep the flow of the narrative in twenty-first-century English. I acknowledge my loving indebtedness to this wonderful biography and to the grace displayed in the conversion of Brownlow North, which grace I have also known.

There is little else written on the life of the evangelist; however, many volumes of Brownlow North's work have been reprinted, all of them photocopies of the original books. As an author, Brownlow North is principally known for his book of messages on words of the Lord Jesus Christ in the Gospel of Luke, originally titled as *The Rich Man and Lazarus: A Practical Exposition of Luke 16:19–31* and later as *A Great Gulf Fixed: A Practical Exposition of Luke 16:19–31*. This was a compilation of sermons that North preached during the Great Awakening in Ulster in 1859.

He also wrote *Ourselves*, a series of eighteen sermons from the book of Exodus concerning the children of Israel's journey out of Egypt and through the wilderness on their way to the land of Canaan. He wrote a companion volume of a series of messages on the parable of Jesus, *The Prodigal Son, or The Way Home*. Then North wrote *Yes! Or No! or God's Way of Salvation*, thirteen sermons on Genesis 24. North also wrote *You! What You Are, and What You May Be*, a series of sermons on the liberation of the demon-possessed man of Gadara. Also in North's expository series of books was *Wisdom: Her Cry*, which were evangelistic Bible readings on Proverbs 1. He produced a little book of messages titled *God's Way of Salvation*, which discussed the beginning of days and how salvation is by the life and blood of Christ rather than our own works of righteousness.

North also gathered together twenty-four of the tracts that he had written over the years, titling the compilation *Gathered Leaves*. These were marvelously straight, direct statements of the New Testament message under headings such as "God Is," "You May Be Saved," "A Thought for the Careless," "The Infidel's Hope," and "How Long Have You Lived?" Similar, briefer books included *Words for the Anxious* and *Think! Earnest Words for the Thoughtless*.

Brownlow North was deeply persuaded about the usefulness of his published sermons, believing that they would go where he could not, and so he produced a book titled *Earnest Words, New and Old*. In the preface he explained

why he had come to write it, expressing his faith in the
importance of the written word:

> Having reason to believe, from the testimony of
> many, that several of the papers in the little book
> called *Earnest Words* have been honoured by God,
> and made useful to souls, I have determined to pre-
> pare a new edition. In it I have retained the articles
> which I think the Lord has been pleased to bless;
> altering and adding to them, however, so as in my
> judgment to improve their likelihood of general use-
> fulness: and in the place of some of the old papers
> I have substituted new. I have also to the end of
> every chapter, in this edition, added a text and a lit-
> tle prayer, and have added a seventh to my "Six Short
> Rules for Christians."
>
> My object in preparing this edition has been to
> produce a comprehensive, plain-spoken, yet cheap
> book, suited for circulation amongst all classes; a
> book having in it which, under God's blessing, might
> awaken the careless, instruct the anxious, and even
> feed the Christian; and knowing that whatever the
> new matter might be, the old has already been made
> effectual for all of these things, I am anxious that this
> edition should be very extensively circulated. I have
> written no book that I would rather see in the hands
> of the multitude, because I have written no book
> which I believe more likely to be generally useful.

Very few of his other books have been reprinted,
but Christian fascination with the extant works of such
nineteenth-century writers as M'Cheyne, Bonar, Hodge,
Spurgeon, and Ryle means that the rediscovery of the leg-
acy of Brownlow North's surviving books cannot be far off.